Is God Finished With Israel?

—ₘ—

By Alan Turner

Michael Stoyke www.yfoto.de
Werner Hostettler w.hostettler@gmail.com

PRESS

Cover Art Design: Michael Stoyke, Berlin, Germany.

Is God Finished With Israel?
by Alan Turner
Web site: members.shaw.ca/menorah

Printed in the United States of America

ISBN 978-1-60647-834-9

www.xulonpress.com

FOREWORD

—ɯ—

Unfortunately, most, if not all, modern-day Christians are completely unaware of the concept of "Replacement Theology" and are, therefore, completely satisfied with whatever might be said about the subject from the preachers they respect, which is often little or nothing. It is my guess that few, if any, have ever heard a message using the title of Alan's book—"Is God Finished with Israel?"—consequently, few, other than the Jews themselves, have even a faint interest in this most-important subject.

As you are reading this Forward, you can count yourself among the elite few, who are about to have the scales removed from the eyes of their understanding and not only have their interest amplified, but also their awareness heightened. In my mind, this is, therefore, a very important day in your life. When one is deceived he/she does not know it; however, when truth comes, the deception is made evident, and, I must add, this is a good thing, a very good thing.

If it is a question of understanding the heart of what Alan Turner has attempted to say in his book, then the title is not difficult even for the simplest of thinkers. For multitudes in this world, to read the five words of Alan's title would excite a genocidal passion which could not come quick enough; to another approximate fourteen million, the very thought of those five words would be an assault on a belief whose roots lie in the beginnings of Bible history; to millions of others composing the mosaic of Christian belief, these five words, arguably, divide the believers into one of the two aforesaid camps.

The author's mission is to answer his question in a very simple and understandable way, in the belief, hope and prayer that God will use this book to replace the lie with His Truth. Only then, in the light of the author's conservative embrace of the Bible as God's authoritative Truth, will you, as the reader, be able to discern aright, and know in your heart, if God is finished with Israel.

I have known the author for more years than he would care for me to admit, and I know more about him than I would dare to admit, but I will admit this: I have never known another, who loves Israel and her people any more passionately than does Alan Turner.

- Mac Goddard, Pastor, Grace Christian Fellowship,
Macon Georgia, USA

TABLE OF CONTENTS

—〰—

ABOUT THE AUTHOR

—ᴍ—

A lan Turner is 'a man for all seasons'. Born and educated
in Bournemouth, England, he is a 'baby-boomer' whose
career yearning towards professional soccer or theatre took a
180-degree turn. Raised in a middle class, religious home, he
was recognized in early teens to be a 'boy preacher'. After
becoming a Christian in early life, he grew to grasp the mega
difference between 'religion' and 'Christianity'.

He regards his time at the London Bible College in
England as "three of the best years of my life." Its diverse
international and inter-denominational infrastructure
prepared him for 'all seasons' in both the secular and spiritual world. As a consequence, he has traveled and preached
in 16 countries.

Alan Turner grew through childhood and adolescence
unaware of the extent of the emotional rejection which was
his. Belonging to a large band of British Second World War
'baby-boomers' he grew up in a typical,English middle
class environment.....unconscious as to the depth of pain
incurred in being a 'love cripple' . Discovering this truth
in later life had not prevented his hurt......nor the hurt he
inflicted on others.

Hurt people hurt people!

On the positive side, he testifies to such rejection as an
identification with Israel and the Jewish people. He has also

seen it as a necessary experience enabling him to embrace the 'amazing grace of God in forgiveness'. As Israel; so Alan!

He is father to three married children, Rachel, Anna, and Joel, and grandfather to seven. When not flying Alan resides in Courtenay, Vancouver Island, British Columbia, Canada.

ALL invitations to Alan for speaking engagements can be channelled via the *Menorah Web Site at*: members.shaw. ca/menorah   or via *Email*: menorah@shaw.ca

DEDICATION

—◊◊◊—

Sha'ul (Paul), the Jewish teacher and writer, in a letter he wrote to the Christian Church in Rome, once asked, "Did God reject his people? By no means! I am an Israelite myself, a descendant of Abraham. If the rejection of Israel is the reconciliation of the world, what will their acceptance be, but life from the dead?" **(Romans 11:1 & 15)**

I dedicate this book to all the Jewish people through the centuries who have suffered horrifically from the words and deeds of those who followed Jesus or, as is the greater truth, those who merely *professed to.*

I dedicate it *to Love; to the God who is Love...* as He continues His eternal preparations from the Cross for *the* most unusual, and miraculous wedding in human history - that of a Jewish and Christian Bride, to a Jewish and Christian Bridegroom!

ACKNOWLEDGEMENTS

—⚡︎—

I assume the very fact I am expressing gratitude on this page must indicate this book is nearing completion, and obviously is a finished work, by virtue of the fact you are reading it !

Displaying a greater confidence in my ability than I myself have, according to some friends this book is 25 years overdue! I personally believe it is 1700years overdue! However, I determined to abide by the example of the late 20th century prophet, Francis Schaeffer, who never wrote a word until he was 50 years of age. Even now at 61 years of age, I wonder what I can possibly contribute which will be used of HaShem (God) to bless His people – both Jew and Gentile.

In the first place I give thanks for my parents, Geoff and Nancy Turner, who dragged me screaming into my first Sunday School, and for the matriarchal grandmother whose prayers were probably instrumental in getting me there.

For the Christian-based family of the Boys' Brigade whose Object showed me there was a godly manliness available as a 1960's lifestyle alternative. To my 'spiritual father', the late Ken Webber, who epitomized that manliness.

To Jean, whose love ,faithfulness, prayers and morality were breaths of the Messiah Himself. I was not worthy of you.

To the three wonderful children born of that love: Rachel, Anna and Joel. I was unprepared... and unworthy to be their father... yet privileged and honoured beyond description to possess that role. They walk with God as adults...and for that alone, I am so grateful to God.

To the late Dr. Doug Roberts, who, reluctantly on my part, became my hero and mentor the day he told me "Alan, you're as phoney as a three dollar bill!" I will forever thank God for that man.

To my own 'spiritual child', landlady and friend, Catherine Bell - thanks for loyally tolerating my baggage! You are a true friend.

To the late Derek Prince.....a preacher who fed this preacher manna from heaven.

To the 'brave few' whom I call friends, unsung heroes who have stayed the course with this eccentric stubborn writer, and dared to believe in me:

Dr.David and Carol Darmstadt; John Grady; Ernie and Connie Kratofil;; Bill and Rachel Millward; Andy Crouch; Andy Couch; Jim Schutz, Frank Woods, Francine Christophersen, Miles White....many others I have inevitably and regrettably omitted.

.To my close friend in the ministry of Grace, Mac Goddard, my personal pastor, and oft 'conscience'. Though the zaniest of characters, he is the finest counsellor I know.

I would be remiss not to mention Malcolm Hedding, Director of the International Christian Embassy in Jerusalem. It is Malcolm, I believe, who is more qualified to write this book than I, having previously demonstrated his author-skills in the area of the same subject.

Penultimately, an incalculable debt of gratitude to my 'co-authors': Corinne Okell, my manuscript writer; Michael Stoyke of Germany for a fabulous front cover photograph; my dear friend Werner Hostettler of Switzerland, for the back cover;....you guys, I can never repay you. Thank you.

Last, but never least, to the One who said, "The last shall be first," my inadequate gratitude forever for Your love, mercy and grace – Yeshua Ha Massiach, Jesus the Messiah of Israel, and Saviour of the World. Where would I be without your forgiveness? I dedicate the message of this book to Your Glory.

PREFACE

—〜〜—

When something happens that has not occurred in one thousand eight hundred and seventy one years, it is worth recording.

Since the destruction of Jerusalem in A.D. 70 by the armies of the Roman emperor Titus, and the ultimate dispersion from the Holy Land in A.D. 135 of all but a handful of Jews, the "wandering Jew" has traversed the far-flung corners of the globe.

Two millennia have passed and, at the commencement of this 21st century, there are once again more Jews living in Israel than in any other place on earth.

On my third visit to Israel in 1982, it came as a great shock to discover that *not* one Jew in Israel was living in the same land as his grandfather lived. Similarly, *not* one Jew in a thousand was speaking the same language his grandfather spoke!

What had happened? What was the significance of this? Whatever it was, and is, it is unprecedented in history! There has been a *complete reversal* of the fortunes of God's ancient people. It is nothing short of *miraculous*.

It happened in two years – just ten years apart – both within the lifetime of my parents – one in mine.

In 1938, then U.S. President Franklin Delano Roosevelt convened an international conference at St. Evian, on the shore of Lake Geneva, Switzerland. The topic was "How do we rescue God's ancient people from the claws of Hitler's predatory Nazi animals?" (Roosevelt did not quite word it in this fashion; this writer has no hesitation in doing so!)

Thirty-two nations were represented at the conference. Only *three* small nations responded practically to America's call: Denmark, Holland and the Dominican Republic. Even the mighty United States itself, conveners of the conference, inexplicably refused to take any Jews.

God 'attended' the conference, so did Nazi Germany. Gestapo observers went back to Hitler and reported, "Nobody wants them…you can do what you want with them now!"

One month later, November 13 and 14, 1938 "KRISTALLNACHT" occurred. It became known as "The Night of the Broken Glass."

It was a night Hitler ordered the destruction of Jewish businesses, vandalism against Jewish stores, the herding of Jewish people for registration, and the ultimate humiliation of this people in the forcible wearing of the yellow star of David. By this act alone, the Jews stood out in the world as being 'different' human beings.

Previously in 1933, Hitler had decided that Jews in Germany were to wear a brand, and that brand would be known as 'The Jew Star' (the insulting name for the Star of David). On the colour, the Nazi's did not have to think very long. Historical significance itself determined it had to be yellow. This colour had been common in a negative and stigmatizing way to Jews for centuries already. The Nazi's even spoke of 'jew yellow'. On May 2, 1942, the yellow Jew star was 'introduced' in the Netherlands. During the years 1933 to 1945, the yellow Star of David therefore fulfilled an unthinkable negative function. In contrast, the Zionistic Star of David was blue on a white background, inspired by the Tallit, the blue and white Jewish prayer cloak. It was blue in fulfillment of Verses 38and39 in the Bible Book of Numbers Chapter 15:-

"The Lord said to Moses,'Speak to the Israelites and say to them: Throughout the generations to come you are to make tassels on the corners of your garments, with a blue cord on each tassel. You will have these tassels to look at and so you will remember all the commands of the Lord ".

Kristallnacht was expunged from the history books for many years.

At that time, the South African Prime Minister queried Hitler concerning the future welfare of the Jews. Hitler wrote back, "The Jews will disappear."

The second integral date was May 14, 1948, ten years forward. The United Nations debated the issue of a national homeland for the Jewish people. It was favourably passed by a majority of one - ironic at the time it was the vote of the Soviet Union!

SO, by a majority of only one vote Palestine became Israel once again after more than 2,000 years of Jewish exile. It is unlikely one will ever read a copy of Time Magazine without at least two pages being devoted to Israel in every issue.

After Hitler's infamous 'final solution' to what he called "the Jewish problem," the remnant of Jews still alive, whose ancestry had found protection for 2,000 years by dispersion, believed that the illusion of freedom was once, and for all, shattered!

Nazism's 20th century systematization of anti-Semitism had created the most heinous method of extermination. Allied with modern technology, it virtually destroyed an entire race in the gas chambers of Europe.

At least two-thirds of the total Jewish population on the planet, died there.

Following the Holocaust, only two large centres of Jewish life remained – the United States and Israel (or Palestine, as

it was known in 1945). In every Jewish centre of population, numbers have markedly decreased. Only in Israel has it
increased, and that, quite remarkably.

I believe the real reason for the growth of Israeli population is owing to four major factors:

* First, the demise of communism in Europe.
* Second, the disintegration of the former Soviet
  Union.
* Third, the demolition of the Berlin Wall.
* Last but not least, the heart-cry of the "Wandering
  Jew" to fulfill his yearning, "Next Year in Jerusalem,"
  the toast at virtually every Jewish gathering.

Coupled with what can only be described as the miracle
of Jewish restoration to the land of Israel is the fact that this
people returned, not only to a "lost" homeland, but also to a
"lost" language. Ancient Hebrew was a language that "died"
after the first century dispersion of the Jewish people. It was
only revived through the brilliance of a man named Eliezer
Ben Yehuda at the end of the 19th century.

Its revival was the first occasion in known history that this
kind of linguistic death and resurrection had ever happened
with any native language.

The multitudes of Jews who have made "aliyah" (the
journey to a new homeland in Israel) have had to learn
modern Hebrew in order to survive in a new country. Thanks
to Ben-Yehuda (1858-1922), a Lithuanian Jew, thousands of
new immigrants coming into the Land have both blessed this
man for his amazing work and, at the same time, "cursed"
him that in order to survive effectively in the new land, it was
paramount they assimilate the language of Israel - Hebrew..

But, we may well ask, "What has any or all of this to do
with a Gentile Theological Doctrine, commonly referred to
as 'Replacement Theology'"?

As we proceed, we shall see that it has *everything* to do with it.

The miracle of the restoration of Israel to its Land in the 20th century is nothing less than the fulfillment of the words of ancient Biblical prophets. Men who not only told forth, but who also foretold. Men, and indeed women, who received their divine revelations from the God of Abraham, Isaac and Jacob. By that same divine spirit, they are enabled to be read and understood by the masses today.

Generally speaking, the Church of Jesus Christ has failed to grasp the truth that the God of Abraham, Isaac and Jacob IS the God of the Church, and that, in this sense; they are 'with us' today.

Failure to comprehend, accept, and believe the plain, basic, direct teaching of the Bible, is the cancerous root lying at the base of the Church's belief in what is called **Replacement Theology**. It is a belief which has permeated the thinking of the Church for over seventeen hundred years!

My humble attempt, in what I trust is a simple book, is merely to introduce and awaken you to the subject. Your belief or unbelief in these truths is solely the responsibility of you, the reader.

INTRODUCTION

—〰—

I t was a relatively unknown Jewish man from Boca Raton, on Florida's east coast, who first approached me in 1991, and literally nagged me to put my public preaching and teaching into print. I had never written anything until that time, save some poetry and newspaper articles. I was not overly enthusiastic about the project, I must admit. Melvin Cohen was not only enthusiastic, he was insistent and persistent! In hindsight, I am glad he was.

We met for lunch, and he quite vociferously and unapologetically pressured me into writing on the subject of Replacement Theology.

Being a qualified 'cheapskate', I relented, especially when he declared he would foot all bills appertaining to printing and production! This in itself was sufficient stimulation for me to begin to apply myself to territory new and unchartered – the **written** word.

Nevertheless, I held some deep reservations about my qualification to write on the particular subject of Replacement Theology. These primarily revolved around my own insecurities, both as a novice writer, and as a failed academic. Added to which was a very poignant objection - I was Gentile (Goy) and Mel Cohen was Jewish!

Although I had taught these truths for over 20 years, I could never feel what he felt about the past and present plight of his people. I won the battle with him on this point, but I lost the war. I 'lost' because Mel knew that anti-Semitism fuelled amongst professing Christians, aroused my righteous anger (and sometimes my anger was not always 'righteous'!)

Within the realm of Christendom, the teaching governing 'Christian anti-Semitism' rhetoric and action, is known as Replacement Theology. My reading of church history would convince me that a more appropriate and truthful description would be '**Religious** anti-Semitism'. There was definitely nothing *Christian* or *Christ-like* in the behaviour of those who through the centuries persecuted the Jewish people.

Replacement Theology postulates a belief system that the Land of Israel and its Jewish population have never possessed any significant importance since the life and time of Jesus Christ.

Coupled with the generally held indictment by 'christians' against Jews, that the latter were THE 'Christ-killers', this often subconscious belief permeated religious and Christian thinking for almost two millennia. I purposely write 'christian' with a small 'c' and inverted commas, as it is my doubt that these people were true Christians at all. I am just glad that HE is 'the Judge of all men', and not me.

Replacement Theology also teaches that whatever historical importance Israel may have held in the past (before Christ), is now no longer tenable. Israel's importance has now been superseded by the birth of the Christian Church.

The emergence on the world scene of the latter made the need, importance and value of the former *obsolete.*

This doctrine – for, indeed, doctrine it is – has fuelled centuries of hatred toward the Jewish people. Sadly, not only has this scenario <u>not</u> improved for the better over time, it has, in fact, worsened! As we embark upon the 21st century, anti-Semitism, globally, is statistically more rampant than at any previous period of history.

What overcame my fears and reservations about writing on the subject of Replacement Theology was the unequivocal assurance I had of the Call of God on my life. Equally real was the specific divine Call I received in Israel itself, in September 1982.

My family and I had returned to England from Canada in 1981. We affiliated with a team ministry in a church in Guildford, U.K. I had not been back 'home' but three months before being gifted with a ticket to Israel.

I had only once before visited Israel in 1977. With my wife, I had led a tour group of 40 pilgrims from Victoria, British Columbia, Canada. We undertook the "normal" tourist trip; two weeks jumping on and off Egged buses (Israel's national bus company). Except we ran where Jesus walked!

In September 1982, a lady in our Guildford church came up to me after I had preached and said, "Alan, I don't know why, but God has told me to buy you a ticket to Israel! I believe He not only wants you to experience the Feast of Tabernacles (FOT)[1] but also to serve in the Feast as a volunteer."

Two consecutive years, two consecutive 'freebies' – too much grace!

The convener and organizer of this spectacular international celebration is the International Christian Embassy, Jerusalem (ICEJ). The Feast and its celebrations is massive in its modus operandi, and therefore dependant upon the many volunteers who assist in caring for 6-7,000 Christian pilgrims who each year faithfully attend this eight day function in Jerusalem. It is the largest tour group visiting Israel each year. No wonder the Israeli Government annu-

---

[1]   Also known as Sukkot, one of the three major Jewish festivals.

ally endorse the Prime Minister to the task of addressing this largely Christian event.

I may be 'goy' (Gentile), but I have enough 'Scottish' blood in me never to refuse a free offer! So I accepted the lady's kindness with deep gratitude.

With the blessing of my church, I was released for a month to assist the International Christian Embassy, Jerusalem. Such was the commitment of the volunteers, our preparations were rewarded by the Director giving all of us two or three days free time prior to the commencement of the 1982 event.

I had heard about a certain resort in Galilee, and it had piqued my carnal mind. Apparently, from this place, one could horse-ride the Galilee at sunset, eat the finest barbequed steaks outside of the U.S., and bunk in chalets constructed wholly in natural pine. Coming from the 'timber capital' of the world in Canada, I was looking forward to being at 'home'.

Back-packing, I left the tourist town of Tiberias, on Lake Galilee's southern shore at around the dinner hour. Winding my way toward the Golan Heights, my eyes were focused in search of this seeming oasis in the wilderness. With a Hebrew name of Vered HaGalil ('Rose of Galilee'), who would not want to experience its amenities?

Unlike my adopted homeland of British Columbia, Canada, dusk descends quite fast in Northern Israel. By nightfall, I was reduced to 'Shanks's pony' (walking) again. I was running out of time. It was almost dark (road lighting was rare in Galilee in those days), and still no indication of my intended goal. In the Providence of God, I was not meant to find Vered Ha Galil that day.

I recognized the road sign leading eastward to the lake's edge – 'Mount of Beatitudes and Hospice', it read. I had experienced this 'holy place' with my tour group in 1977, only then, I did not require a bed for the night.

The hospice was staffed by Italian nuns. None (excuse the pun) could converse in English, or even colloquial Hebrew! It was a lonely experience and not at all what I had originally and excitedly looked forward to.

Being the sole sojourner that night, I retired early. I lay on my bed doing what I do best – thinking.

Maybe I was succumbing to the trap of the centuries, dwelling on the negatives of the past, and becoming crippled in the present. Whatever it was, or was not, I had for many years felt myself to be a dysfunctional emotional cripple as the result of my upbringing.

Suddenly my life was changed forever. I heard an audible voice, but I saw no one. I sat bolt upright on the bed. The voice called my name a second time. I opened the door and surveyed the hallway – nobody there. Returning to the room, I looked through the bedroom window, no sign of life in the night outside. I peered into the bathroom; as empty as when I had recently vacated it. In my utter frustration, I looked under the bed - just the same dust and cobwebs that probably accompanied the last guest.

I heard my name for the third time. Only by now, in fear and trepidation, I was in the Presence of the very same One who had called Samuel to be a prophet over 3,000 years earlier.

"Alan, my son, the rejection you have experienced in your life is but an infinitesimal portion of what My People Israel has experienced through the centuries. But it is a necessary pre-requisite for the work to which I am about to call you." Silence! I was speechless.

Arguably, for the first time in thirty-five years, I was a man without words!

My overnight stay passed without further interruption. I did not need any more excitement in one night, particularly as it all seemed so irrational to my cerebral thinking.

Confused and perplexed, I returned the next day to Jerusalem. The spirit of joy, praise and wonder which resonates during the Christian Celebration of the Jewish Feast of Sukkot, pre-occupied my body, soul and spirit for the next eight days.

Only on returning to England, and Providentially meeting new friends, would I discover what my Galilee experience was all about.

I do not know to this day how the Lord put four strangers together, each of whom had, in recent months, individually found in his heart a brand new, inexplicable, love for the Land and people of Israel.

What could men of different personalities, cultures and ages possibly hold in common? One of the men was a retired tax collector, one a church pastor, one a London bank manager, along with the Anglo- Canadian new boy - me.

The glue which united us was two-fold. Our salvation and common faith in Jesus Christ, and our new found love for Israel and the Jewish people.

We met regularly every Monday night to heed the Biblical injunction to "pray for the peace of Jerusalem." (**Psalm 122:6**). During that year of 1982/3, I learnt *two* important things about my 'Galilee experience'.

First, I understood the meaning of the Jewish candlestick, the Menorah. It became the umbrella sign by which God was about to change the emphasis of my Bible teaching. Having been raised as a conservative evangelical, imagine what I was going through in my own self-examination. One thing I was certain of, the name *menorah* was definitely not in my Bible!

God began to show me the Jewish roots of my Bible and faith. I had never even 'heard' of these truths, let alone understood them. Of course, I knew them as background facts to the coming of Jesus, but *not* as facts relevant to the past or present Church-Age.

Only the rhema (revelation word) voice of God to my spirit, and the subsequent teaching he gave me from His logos (written word) enabled me to assimilate into my understanding that, as a Gentile Christian preacher, it would be acceptable for me to embark on a 'new' ministry. A ministry which now included exhorting Christians to 'comfort Israel' and 'pray for the peace of Jerusalem'.

Second, I came to understand that my belief system was known by a certain title. Being a Christian who has long despised 'labels', I was not too enamoured with this. However, it is difficult in our world to live without labels and, as time wore on, I came to realize I had indeed become a **'Christian Zionist'**. As my Biblical studies delved deeper, I came to embrace and cherish this new revelation from the Lord.

Long-standing friends, worldwide, and especially those with evangelical persuasion, remonstrated with me in loving fashion. Their protestations were so marked, I began to wonder if I had fallen into apostasy. Had I affiliated with a kind of 'Jonestown, Guyana' cult[2]? Had I, for all my avowed dogmatic conservatism, suddenly gone off the rails and become a heretic?

Would I be 'burnt at the stake' as it were, and be ostracized by the Body of Christ on earth? Would the doors close forever against my itinerant preaching?

All of these thoughts, and more, preoccupied my thinking and definitely my praying. If I felt rejected before, that rejection would be exacerbated from this time on.

---

[2] James Warren "Jim" Jones (1931 – 1978) was the American founder of the Peoples Temple. Over 900 people died on November 18, 1978 in a mass murder-suicide by poison. It was orchestrated by Jones as the community was named by him, and after him.

Well-meaning pastor/preacher colleagues entreated me to 'return to the fold', what they referred to as the 'conservative Biblical orthodoxy' fold.

All the time, my inner spirit was gaining strength and my mind was being taught new lessons from old truths.

As a young man, along with the majority of Christendom, I had been raised in my particular church hearing teaching such as: "The Church has superseded Judaism"; "When Christ came, God no longer had a purpose for Israel"; "Israel is now obsolete"; "The prophecies are no longer relevant"; and to cap them all, "The Church has replaced Israel."

I was only now beginning to discover such teaching had been the vertebrae of what is commonly called *Replacement Theology*. The ramifications of this doctrine have abounded for almost two millennia.

Adherence to it has been at the heart of all thoughts and subsequent actions of oppression, aggression, harassment and war against the Jewish people. This would be true not only in the land of Palestine, but also in heavily populated Jewish centres throughout the world.

I would like to report that anti-Semitism ceased with the formation of the modern State of Israel in 1948. Instead, this miraculous event served only to accentuate the hatred levelled against Jesus' descendants in the flesh.

Historically, *Replacement Theology* had fuelled hatred and animosity. It had incited numerous attempts at genocide over 1,700 years. It had poisoned the minds of professing Christian people over that time period. It lies behind the reason the majority of Christian churches are more in sympathy with the so-called 'Palestinian cause' than in seeing God's Word fulfilled in the nation of Israel.

It is to the subject of *Replacement Theology* I address this book. It is not intended to be a masterpiece or even the ultimate authority on the subject. It is, I trust, simply written that even a child may understand some of its salient truth. If I have failed here, I have failed as a writer!

I dedicate this book to the memory of the six million... the memory of countless lives lost to Israel's mothers since 1948...to the Arab Israelis who, by the grace of the Israeli Jew, share the land with their Jewish cousins...and to the Christian Zionists who seek only to uphold and defend the basic inerrancy of God's Holy Word – known to us as 'The Bible'."

CHAPTER 1

REPLACEMENT THEOLOGY IS NEITHER A NEW OR "NEW AGE" TEACHING

—⟋ɯ⟍—

The essence of a belief in Replacement Theology has permeated the thoughts and belief of the followers of Jesus Christ since the embryonic days of Christianity.

To put it simply and succinctly, belief in Replacement Theology is a belief that 'the universal church of Jesus Christ has become Israel'. It is commonly and erroneously referred to as 'the New Israel', a term not used anywhere in the Bible.

There can be little doubt in the mind of even a novice Bible student, Israel enjoyed a special and unique relationship with God according to the Bible. This appertained to both her destiny as a nation and the messages God gave to her prophets concerning a national homeland.

Replacement Theology teaches that, since the first Pentecost, all this has now been negated in the light of Israel's rejection of the Messiahship of Jesus.

I referred earlier to the Church's new title for this belief system – the "Israel of God" or "the New Israel" – thus inferring that the Church is now the sole expression of the entirety of God's purpose on the earth. In other words, the Church is the historic continuation of Israel.

It negates God's original call and commission to Abram (Abraham) as the father and head of both a new race (the Jews), and a faith-race (the Church).

According to this thinking, the Jewish people are therefore no different from all other people, such as the Canadians, French, Japanese or, for that matter, any other race on earth. All these peoples need salvation in Jesus Christ – the Jews are no different. With this statement the writer is in total agreement - it is indeed what Scripture clearly teaches in Galatians 3:28, "There is neither Jew nor Greek, slave nor free, male nor female..."

When it comes to the matter of salvation in and through the merit of the finished work of Jesus Christ upon the Cross- ALL peoples stand as individual human beings before God, regardless of religion, race or respectability!

However, let us understand further. Replacement Theology consequentially declares that apart from repentance, new birth and entrance into the Church, the Jews have no future, no hope and no calling as a distinct race of people.

The Church now inherits the blessings once promised to the nation of Israel, yet, the judgments and curses are retained solely for the Jewish people. In essence, this is the defining doctrine known as Replacement Theology.

For the remainder of this Chapter by way of illustration and elaboration, I will be drawing upon the writings of my dear friend Malcolm Hedding (with his full acknowledgement and permission, I might add).

Malcolm (Director of the International Christian Embassy, Jerusalem) has shrewdly observed, "One of the factors that led to the birth of Replacement Theology was an historical one. This teaching was conceived at a time in history when

'Israel curses' are retained for the Jewish people."[3] This is the kernel of understanding which has prompted this writer's response to the question, "Is God Finished with Israel?"

This teaching was conceived at a time in history when Israel as a nation was in dispersion. The Land of Canaan was barren, infertile, and her cities, especially Jerusalem, were mere desert outposts. It seemed beyond belief that the Land could ever again be restored to its former glory.

The challenge to the proponents of Replacement Theology is how they deal with what is nothing less than a miracle – the re-birth of the modern state of Israel in 1948, and the subsequent return of the Jewish people to their Land, the fulfillment of no less than 141 Biblical prophecies! It has happened! The vast array of God-given promises in Scripture HAS been fulfilled, and the 21st century adherents of Replacement Theology do not know what to do with fulfilled prophecy. With the help of the Holy Spirit, it is the purpose of this book to navigate such minds and then furnish them with truth enabling them to comprehend this 20th century 'miracle'.

Christians who believe these definite Biblical prophecies concerning Israel, and acknowledge God's sovereign hand of grace and mercy upon this people, identify themselves with God's infallible Word. Whether such Christians lay claim to any title or not, their open and unashamed stance with the Jewish people would label them 'Christian Zionists'. It is not a political movement. It could easily be called 'Biblical Christian Zionism'. It is not a calling to Christians to be even a political voice for Israel, but rather, a prophetic voice for God.

As Malcolm Hedding declares, "Christian Zionism seeks to declare the truth of God's Word that bequeaths to the

---

[3] Malcolm Hedding..."Christian Action for Israel"...4th Quarter ... Newsletter...1999.

people of Israel the land of Canaan as an everlasting possession."[4] Such a promise was made by God to Abraham some
4,000 years ago in Genesis 13:14-18:

> The Lord said to Abram after Lot had parted
> from him, "Lift up your eyes from where you are
> and look north and south, east and west. All the land
> that you see I will give to you and your offspring
> forever. I will make your offspring like the dust of
> the earth, so that if anyone could count the dust, then
> your offspring could be counted. Go walk through
> the length and breadth of the land for I am giving it
> to you." So Abram moved his tents and went to live
> near the great trees of Mamre at Hebron, where he
> built an altar to the Lord.

The God who exiled the Jewish people (on a national
scale) on two occasions (586 B.C. and A.D. 70) has always
promised to bring them back and restore their fortunes again
(there were of course numerous invasions of 'Palestine', and
multitudes of 'mini-exiles' throughout the centuries, but none
of them on the scale of the two periods aforementioned).

"Hear the word of the Lord, O nations, And declare in the
coastlands afar off, And say, 'He who scattered Israel will
gather him and keep him as a shepherd keeps his flock.'"
(Jeremiah 31:10)

"Then it will happen on that day that the Lord will again
recover the *second* time with His hand the remnant of His
people, who will remain, from Assyria, Egypt, Pathros,
Cush, Elam, Shinar, Hamath, and from the island of the sea."
(Isaiah 11:11)

---

[4] Malcolm   Hedding..."Replacement   Theology"...Published   by
Doubleday Consumer Services, Des Plaines,Iowa 60018.

These prophecies and promises referring to the restoration of Israel, along with countless others (as I mentioned earlier, 141 times in the Bible) have everything to do with the heart, nature and character of God himself. The Creator's relationship with his creature (man) has only, ever, and always, been based and built upon COVENANT.

Covenant is a solemn oath or bond by which God made agreements with the people of Israel. This book is not the place to delve deep into this delicate and delicious subject, but, in simplicity, a covenant implies both an unconditional aspect on God's part, and a responsibility upon the part of the recipient.

Most Christians have, at the very least, a vague understanding and appreciation that their salvation in Christ and acceptance into the Kingdom of God is a consequence of the New Covenant.

As prophesied in Jeremiah 31,

celebrated by Jesus himself in Matthew 26:28, and

expounded by the writer to the Hebrews in Chapter 8

However, most do not realize that the New Covenant does not appear, as Malcolm so succinctly declares, "......in a vacuum."

It is the *consequence* of the Abrahamic Covenant which God entered into with this Gentile from Ur of the Chaldees. Most scholars believe Ur lies in the delta of the Persian Gulf, where the two great rivers, Tigris and Euphrates, flow together. If so, this would give credence to the understanding that Abram was from the country currently known as Iraq!

Between Genesis 12 and Genesis 17, God changes Abram's name to Abraham. God breathed His Spirit into both Abram and Sarai (signified by breathing out, like we would say the consonant 'H'), and thus He placed Himself within them.

The name of God's sovereignly elected servant changed, and so did God's declaration of the Covenant. Note in Genesis 15:18, it is referred to as "*a* covenant" but in Genesis 17:2 onwards it becomes "*my* covenant."

God's promises are to a new race of which Abraham is the head; a new race entitled to live in a new land by Divine decree. Abraham is now the progenitor of both a physical race and a spiritual one. An entire Chapter in **Romans 4** is dedicated to the Apostle Paul's confirmation of this four thousand years later! The Covenant itself is to be found in Genesis 12:2-3: "I will make you into a great nation, and I will bless you. I will make your name great and you will be a blessing. I will bless those who bless you; and whoever curses you I will curse. And all peoples on earth will be blessed through you."

It is a 7-fold blessing upon Abram. In blessing No. 6, God puts in a 'protection clause'. Whenever God calls a man, he becomes a major object for cursing and destruction from Lucifer (satan) himself. (If for no other reason, this alone behooves us to pray for the men and women Called of God into Christian leadership.) We have a modern word for 'cursing' Abraham and his seed – it's called 'anti-Semitism'. This horrible word first appeared in 1878 and is a phrase coined by the secular world. It was originally a *racial* word, **not** a *religious* one!

God ratifies this Covenant with Israel in Genesis 17:1-8. As any good and normal thinking father would do, Abraham pits his reason and logic against Divine intelligence and laughs off God's promises. Furthermore, in Verse 18 he makes an understandable plea for God's blessing to be bestowed upon his illegitimate firstborn son, Ishmael. Such is God's amazing grace, not only does Yahweh promise to bless the son of Abram and Hagar, but He also promises him rulership over the twelve tribes of Arabia! As always, God kept His promise, and that blessing, conferred upon Ishmael and his seed, has been fulfilled to this very day.

Whatever differences Sunni and Shi'ite Muslims have with each other, they are ALL bound to one false god (Allah), his false prophet (Mohammed) and one false book, the Koran.

I would not want my exegesis of Scripture to come before you without a complete scrutiny of it on the part of my reader.

This covenant is mentioned extensively in the Bible, in both Old Testament and New. In fact, most believers would be amazed to discover the extent of its teaching in the New Testament.

Let us not forget, the writer of the letter to the Hebrews wrote *after* the Jewish citizens of Palestine (as it was then named by the Romans), had rejected the credentials of Jesus for Messiah.

He writes with certainty and knowledge of God's faithfulness to them in Jesus, because he knew God had been totally faithful to Abraham and the seed of Abraham.

"For when God made the promise to Abraham, since He could swear by no one greater, He swore by Himself, saying, 'I will surely bless you and I will surely multiply you.' And so, having patiently waited, he obtained the promise. For men swear by one greater than themselves, and with them an oath given as confirmation is an end of every dispute. In the same way God, desiring even more to show to the heirs of the promise the unchangeableness of His purpose, interposed with an oath, so that by two unchangeable things in which it is impossible for God to lie, we who have taken refuge would have strong encouragement to take hold of the hope set before us." (Hebrews 6:13-18)

Malcolm Hedding goes so far as to speak adamantly and forcibly, questioning the absence of morality in the Replacement Theology position: "They are," he says "in effect accusing God of lying. They are laying an accusation against the character of God when they claim that the purpose of God for the Jewish people, in terms of a national destiny, in a national homeland, has been removed."[5]

In the final analysis, Replacement Theology contradicts Scripture. It is, in its essence, nothing more than the thinking of men! In its refutation of literal Scripture, it prevents Christian people from understanding God's redemptive purposes.

The truth is:

1. God has *not* cast off national Israel.
2. Canaan, to the present day, is Israel's national homeland.
3. The Church has *not* replaced Israel, she has only enlarged her.
4. The modern restoration of Israel is evidence of God's faithfulness to His Word and promises.

> "Therefore remember that formerly you, the Gentiles in the flesh, who are called "Uncircumcision" by the so-called "Circumcision" which is performed in the flesh by human hands – remember that you were at that time separate from Christ, excluded from the commonwealth of Israel, and strangers to the covenants of promise, having no hope and without God in the world. But now in Christ Jesus you who formerly were far off have been brought near by the blood of Christ." (Ephesians 2:11-13)

---

[5] Malcolm Hedding..."Christian Action for Israel"...4th Quarter... Newsletter...1999.

"But if some of the branches were broken off, and you, being a wild olive, were grafted in among them and became partaker with them of the rich root of the olive tree, do not be arrogant toward the branches; but if you are arrogant, remember that it is not you who supports the root, but the root supports you." (Romans 11:17-18)

5. The restoration of Israel will culminate in the coming of the Messiah. Therefore, the Church is able to see this in the Bible and ready not only herself, but bless Israel and 'comfort her'. (Isaiah 40)
6. The restoration of Israel, including the so-called West Bank, is the first step toward national redemption:

"For I do not want you, brethren, to be uninformed of this mystery – so that you will not be wise in your own estimation – that a partial hardening has happened to Israel until the fullness of the Gentiles has come in; and so all Israel will be saved; just as it is written, 'The deliverer will come from Zion, He will remove ungodliness from Jacob.' This is my covenant with them, when I take away their sins." (Romans 11:25-27)

This writer has been asked countless times by fellow Christians, "How do you share the Gospel (the Good News) with Jewish people who do not accept the New Testament?" My answer is simple. I only major upon speaking with them from THEIR Scriptures!

My fellow believer, the truth is simple, study to know the Old Testament Scriptures.

If the salvation of people (be they Jew or Gentile) means anything to us at all, surely it is a small price to

pay in order to be efficient in communicating the Good
News of the Messiah (Christ)?

I will never forget my third visit to Israel in 1982. My
new Israeli friend, Avigdor owned a brass shop in Jerusalem.
At the time of writing he still does. We played soccer together
in Jerusalem's Sacher Park on the eve of every Sabbath. I had
begged him for the opportunity to meet some of his friends
over a Jewish meal. He arranged it one evening after work in
the back room of a friend's store (for security reasons).

We were huddled in this tiny place feasting on hummus,
pita, olives, salad and chicken. I found myself scrunched on
a dirty sack of waste paper in a corner talking with this beau-
tiful Jewish girl in her mid-20's. The conversation became
deep.

Eventually she asked me why I believed Yeshua (Jesus)
was the Jewish Messiah. I opened my pocket Bible to Isaiah
53, where it reads:

Who has believed our message and to whom has
the arm of the Lord been revealed? He grew up before
him like a tender shoot, and like a root out of dry
ground. He had no beauty or majesty to attract us to
him, nothing in his appearance that we should desire
him. He was despised and rejected by men, a man of
sorrows, and familiar with suffering. Like one from
whom men hide their faces he was despised, and we
esteemed him not.

Surely he took up our infirmities and carried our
sorrows, yet we considered him stricken by God,
smitten by him, and afflicted. But he was pierced for
our transgressions, he was crushed for our iniquities; the punishment that brought us peace was upon
him, and by his wounds we are healed. We all, like
sheep, have gone astray, each of us has turned to his

own way; and the Lord has laid on him the iniquity of us all. He was oppressed and afflicted, yet he did not open his mouth; he was led like a lamb to the slaughter, and as a sheep before her shearers is silent, so he did not open his mouth. By oppression and judgement he was taken away. And who can speak of his descendants? For he was cut off from the land of the living; for the transgression of my people he was stricken. He was assigned a grave with the wicked, and with the rich in his death, though he had done no violence, nor was any deceit in his mouth. Yet it was the Lord's will to crush him and cause him to suffer, and though the Lord makes his life a guilt offering, he will see his offspring and prolong his days, and the will of the Lord will prosper in his hand. After the suffering of his soul, he will see the light of life, and be satisfied; by his knowledge my righteous servant will justify many, and he will bear their iniquities. Therefore I will give him a portion among the great, and he will divide the spoils with the strong, because he poured out his life unto death, and was numbered with the transgressors. For he bore the sin of many, and made intercession for the transgressors.

I showed her how my Saviour (Messiah) had come, lived, died, and rose again, all in fulfillment of her own Jewish Scriptures.

The simplicity of her pronouncement in response 'blew' my doubting mind away. So much so, I will never forget that experience. "Well, that's simple," she replied, "I can believe that!"

I have never seen that young lady since, but I have not one iota of doubt she responded to the overtures of Yahweh (Israel's God) in accord with His Covenant made with His Son, Yeshua....Israel's prophesied Messiah .

I would be naïve if I stated evangelism, "is always that easy"; it is not! But neither is it always that difficult!

A Jewish Rabbi once said to me, " Do you realise you and I are only separated by 72 hours of history ! " How profound!

One of the great and legendary saints in the Orthodox Church of England, Bishop J.C. Ryle, Bishop of Liverpool (1815-1900), once said: "I warn you, that unless you interpret the prophetical portion of the Old Testament in a simple literal meaning of its words, you will find it no easy matter to carry on a debate with a Jew. Will you dare tell him that Zion, Jerusalem, Jacob, Judah, Ephraim, Israel, do NOT mean what they seem to mean, but mean the Church of Christ instead?"

To arrive at such a belief system could somewhat be understood in the light of the fact that only a tiny minority of Jewish people actually embrace the divinity and messiahship of the historical Jesus of Nazareth.

However, it is important to remember it <u>was</u>, indeed, Jewish disciples predominantly and not Gentiles who embraced this Nazarene and his teachings at the birth of the Church.

Nevertheless, after Christianity had been declared the universal religion of the then Roman Empire (an edict issued in A.D. 326 by the Emperor Constantine), numerically the Christian Church grew exponentially by the influx of Gentile converts.

These new believers became followers of Jesus converted to Him from other belief systems. They followed Him departing from pantheism, agnosticism, Gnosticism and, for many, possessing no belief system whatsoever! The believers in the Church now comprise a predominance of Gentiles over Jews...a fact which has continued throughout church history, of course.

I am persuaded Christian history will record the Roman Emperor Constantine's dictatorial 'evangelistic strategy' as being a hallmark in the positive numerical growth of the Church. However, it created two major negatives, both of which had a profound impact upon Jewish-Christian relations.

First, Constantine's program did not proclaim a Gospel of Grace - an invitation by God Himself to respond to His gift of salvation in Christ. Rather his mandate was one of involuntary surrender to this religion, as religion it, indeed, was.

By religion, I am referring to the original meaning of the Latin word 'religare' – meaning quite simply 'rules and regulations'.

Jesus Christ did not give to the world a command demanding adherence to rules and regulations. Rather, He brought the message of Himself and His Cross – that men and women could be spiritually free within, both for this life and the next.

Jesus entire life of Being, teaching and doing was focused on the mission His Father gave Him - that, through a conscious act of repentance and faith, those whom God called, could enter into a personal relationship with God's Son.

Constantine's 'christian religion' ordered the masses to 'do works in order to earn salvation'. Thus, it was during this period of Church history in which the original idolatrous practices of relics, rosaries, crucifixes and deeds of penance began to predominate in the Roman Catholic Church. Paganism entered in with a flourish. Scripture was ignored and even rejected in favour of the ecclesiastic rules and traditions of men. In other words – religion!

The second negative produced by Constantine's edict concerned the Jewish people themselves. Constantine launched an offensive against the Jewish people which included murder, rape, pillaging and deportations, thus beginning a wave of anti-Semitism which has lasted through seventeen centuries into this present twenty-first millennium.

As far as the majority of Christendom is concerned, the nation of Israel has forfeited her favoured position as 'God's chosen people' if, indeed, she ever was so honoured. From the 4th century A.D. it became entrenched in ecclesiastic (the 'theology' of church structure), religious thinking, that those whom God once spoke to, and through (Israel), were now passed over or 'cast aside'. A new revelation by God had now been given to the world – the life, death and resurrection of Jesus the Nazarene. Somehow it hardly ever occurred to the Church of almost 2.000 years that the Deity it professed to follow was in fact, in His human nature, Jewish.

The inevitable ramification of such a system of belief is, not only has the Church inherited rights, covenants and blessings (for centuries promised to Israel), but, by such a forfeiture of blessing, the converse has in fact occurred. That is, Israel, by virtue of its rejection of Jesus as the Messiah, now inherits all the Biblically prescribed curses!

The logical outcome of the teaching inherently places Israel in a position like any and every other ethnic and racial group before God. In other words, the only place of eternal blessing in God's sight for any Jew on the earth is for him or her to respond to the claims of the Gospel, and be assimilated into the membership and practices of the Christian Church.

I have no argument with the first part of this belief, but I do with the second!

Under Constantine, the church (please note I do not use a capital 'C' on this occasion!) became like a social club. Into its membership, the people brought not only themselves, but also all the vain practices, traditions, unbiblical doctrines, and worldly practices from living constantly under threat of death. The majority of these 'new Christians' were forcibly 'converted' and motivated to become 'Christian' solely out of fear for their lives. Such 'evangelism' was most definitely foreign to the Biblical pattern laid out for us in Scripture.

Neither Jesus, nor the mighty Apostle Paul (Sha'ul), taught that to believe on Jesus of Nazareth necessitated parting from the culture, customs and good traditions of Judaism. Jesus was born a Jew and He died a Jew. WHEN He returns for His Bride, He will return AS a Jew!

Should one of my readers with an astute eye for theological exactitudes sense that he is now reading the writing of an evangelical 'heretic', allow me to elaborate. There is, according to the Bible, no entrance into the Kingdom of God outside of the blood of the Jewish Messiah, Jesus (Yeshua).

However, when the Scriptures talk about national preservation they refer to the nation of Israel exclusively. God has not committed Himself to preserve any other nation in the world. When the Scriptures speak of the Jew, the Apostle Paul (himself a Jew) takes pains to declare that there is "value in every way in being a Jew." (Romans 3:1)

Our contention is that culturally God does not ask a Jew to forsake his Jewishness, rather to fulfill it, or complete it, as did Jesus Himself.

Replacement Theology is more commonly referred to as 'Covenant Theology'. It is a belief that all of God's covenant promises to the nation of Israel have, since the coming of Jesus, now been transferred to the Church.

This writer must be restrained in the expression of his frustration at the frightening reality that intelligent people actually hold to this position. I say this in the light of the fact that I myself was one such subscriber for years! In fact, I had been an avid Bible student for 22 years before God opened the eyes of my understanding. Only after all those years did I identify the teaching – 'The Church is the New Israel' - as being a teaching contrary to Divine Scripture.

Why has Replacement Theology permeated the belief of the Christian Church for so long? As a former Bible College

Dean, I taught my students what I myself was taught – a dictum which, if embraced tenaciously, would stand one on solid ground when engaged in hermeneutics (that is, the study of the methodological principles of interpretation as of the Bible)[6].

A text without a context is a pretext!

Replacement Theology as a body of teaching has been, through the centuries, the natural outflow of a certain method of interpreting Scripture. It is a method used from the earliest days of the writing of the New Testament books – a method referred to as - ALLEGORIZATION.

---

[6] "hermeneutics."..Websters New World Dictionary...3rd College Edition...1988.

CHAPTER 2

ALLEGORICAL OR LITERAL INTERPRETATION

—ᵯ—

Webster's dictionary defines an allegory as "a poem, play, picture, etc. in which the apparent meaning of the characters and events is issued to symbolize a moral or spiritual meaning."

In recent times, a universally recognized Christian author and theologian, excelling in the art of allegory was C.S. Lewis. Lewis revelled in its use when writing fiction. His classic book, *The Screwtape Letters* demonstrated the use of allegory. Another classic, *The Lion, The Witch and the Wardrobe*, abounded in allegory. The world is particularly cognizant of the latter as the result of its highly successful production as a movie in 2005 entitled *The Chronicles of Narnia*. The movie was arguably successful with respect to the original writer's goal. Lewis definitely conveyed to children the truths of God's sovereignty over creation, evolution, human nature, life, death and resurrection! That mere theatre, portraying the animal kingdom in the realm of fantasy could penetrate the minds of adults as well as children, is testimony to the brilliance of its early 20th century author.

We live in a wonderful world of words, a. sophisticated world. A world which has, since the 1960's, become quite expert at questioning and challenging everything and everyone. The bottom line is, we only have words by which we can effectively communicate. That is, unless we can learn the dictum of the 20th century salesman, "A picture is worth a thousand words." This is what allegory is. It is a picture.

Let me explain. If we speak of a soccer or hockey player being a 'rock' in defence, we are not referring to him as a lump of stone! We mean he plays that hard (as hard as stone)........ so hard he is extremely difficult to beat to the ball or puck.

When Jesus speaks of Himself as, "the bread of life, the vine, the water of life," obviously He is not saying, "I am physical bread, physical wood, physical water." The descriptions He used of Himself correspond to some kind or type of reality. These are metaphors, used much by allegorical writers. Words or phrases ordinarily and primarily used of one thing are applied to another.

One of the most renowned theologians and philosophers of the early Christian church in the 2nd and 3rd centuries was a man named Origen of Alexandria (A.D. 185–254). He was one of the early Church Fathers (leaders). If any one human being was a major influence in the emergence of Replacement Theology into the central doctrine of the Christian faith, it was Origen of Alexandria. Considered one of the Church's greatest theologians, never the less Origen was a major proponent of this teaching. He was largely responsible, not only for its acceptance into the main body of early Church belief, but also its acceptance into the dogma of the Church's mainstream teaching on the subject. Such an introduction would remain an integral aspect of Christian thinking for centuries to come.

It is not without a mountain of historical evidence that we note the correlation between this methodology of teaching, and the 'Christian' anti-Semitism waged against the Jewish people through seventeen centuries. For such anti-Semitism to be confined to mere words would be one thing, but for it to incorporate desecration, devastation, destruction, rape, murder, pillage, hatred and attempted genocide, is something totally other.

Emphatically, no group or race of people in the world has suffered like the Jewish people. Not even the plight of the beleaguered North American native comes that close.

Let us look at a simple illustration of the allegorical method used in seeking to understand Scripture.

There is a passage in the 21st Chapter of the Gospel of Matthew in which the writer relates a certain happening in Jesus' life. It was the occasion of His triumphant entrance into Jerusalem, at the beginning of the final phase of His earthly life. An entrance which was misunderstood by the masses then, and misconstrued by the masses ever since.

The passage speaks of Jesus entering Jerusalem on, "a donkey and the colt of a donkey." I have often endeavoured to picture the Saviour of the world astride both animals at once! However, having observed how closely a foal trots beside its mother, it is much easier to accept the Scriptural narrative in Matthew 21. In fact, all the more so with Jesus' posterior on one animal and his feet gently resting on the other, relaxed, as He always was.

When Origen read Matthew's manuscript he gave to this passage of Scripture what he had applied to many others in his exegesis (an extensive and critical intepretation of an authoritative text)[7] of the Word of God he 'allegorized' it! In other words, he read meaning into the happening, and, in his interpretation, gave an explanation totally other than the

---

[7] "exegesis"..."critical explanation of a text, especially of Scripture"... Oxford Dictionary...2nd Edition ...1996..."

real, literal meaning of the event, which was the description intended and painted by the Gospel writer.

The result was, Origen viewed the 'picture' as demonstrating the two sections of the Bible – Old and New Testaments! The donkey (Old Testament) being older, and therefore more authoritarian - harder, stricter. In contrast, the colt (New Testament)...softer, gentle, more loving - peaceful.

This was the allegory Origen applied often when interpreting Scripture. He totally missed the literal point of literal Scripture – that this passage is purely and simply about Jesus! The praise and adoration of the people was the praise and adoration of Jesus Himself. It had nothing whatsoever to do with donkeys!

To view the Bible from an allegorical perspective is to NOT see it in its literal meaning. Rather it is to analyze its words as mere symbols of a seemingly deeper spiritual meaning or reality.

Therefore, the application of such a method of Biblical interpretation can leave no room for doubting. The ramification of this 'method' tells us, if a donkey can be understood to represent the Old Testament, and the colt of the donkey can represent the New Testament, it is not difficult to understand, how, through the centuries 'Christians' have substituted the Church for the literal nation of Israel when reading Scripture!

I put the word 'Christians' in inverted commas, as I believe that God alone knows the heart. He alone is cognizant of those who are true sons in the faith, and those who are illegitimate.

Origen's use of allegory became the standard acid test for centuries in the Church's approach to hermeneutics (refers to the study of the interpretation of religious texts)[8]. Not

---

[8] "hermeneutics." .."concerning interpretation of, especially Scripture or literary texts"....Oxford Dictionary...2nd Edition...1996

until the 16th century was Origen's system of interpretation challenged. It took the life and devotion of a young German Roman Catholic priest Martin Luther (A.D. 1483–1546) to confront 'allegorization' and argue for a literal interpretation of the Bible.

This priest read the letter of Paul to the Romans. He was gloriously and wonderfully converted, from a life of religious Catholicism, into a personal relationship with Jesus Christ. Historically he is a hero of the Protestant faith. The present-day Church can thank God for his conversion. The legacy of his work and writings have been preserved for over 400 years, and true Bible students in every generation since Luther are grateful.

Believing the Bible should be interpreted literally does not negate the validity of symbolism. The two major prophetic books of Daniel and Revelation dealing with eschatology (a branch of theology concerned with the final events in the history of the world or of humankind)[9] are brim full with symbolism. However, whenever we apply the dictum, "a text without a context is a pretext," it is usually made clear to the reader by the Holy Spirit as to when symbolism is to be understood as symbolism.

As we shall see later, reading symbolism into the innumerable promises of God concerning Israel not only is unacceptable hermeneutics (method of interpretation) but also makes for incoherent and incomprehensible Scripture.

The Bible does indeed flow throughout with a variety of figurative language, poetry and, yes, symbolism. Yet, when we apply the standard rules of grammar – the structure of a sentence, its language, its tense, its context, we understand that the events written about are truly historical. Likewise,

---

[9] "eschatology."..."the part of theology concerned with death and final destiny...that dealing with death ,resurrection ,judgment, immortality"....Oxford Dictionary...2nd Edition...1996..

the predictions made for the future are genuinely literal. They will materialize or else prove to be fraudulent.

At the close of the 20th century we witnessed a proliferation of prophetic writings – Christian, Jewish, religious and secular. The majority wrote much about the post-World War Two generation in particular, often relating it to 'the Messianic Age'.

In Jewish circles alone, there have been recent attempts to place the label 'Messiah' upon the shoulders of more than one prominent Jew; from New York's assassinated Rabbi, Meir Kahane, to the assassinated Prime Minister Yitzhak Rabin, from Henry Kissinger to Ariel Sharon. Yet not one of these, or all combined, can demonstrate Biblical qualification for such pre-eminence!

The Jew, Yeshua (Jesus), alone, meets each and every Biblical criterion.

One Bible scholar discovering Jesus had fulfilled each and every Old Testament prophecy, and not wishing to be only one of a multitude discovering the same truth, calculated the chances of only one man fulfilling ALL the prophecies of Messiahship as 633 to the power of 10! This figure being so astronomical, it borders on infinity! Surprise, surprise!

No genuine professing Christian would even consider 'allegorizing' Scripture when it comes to interpreting the passages which speak of the Person of Jesus.

Bible passages such as Isaiah 7:14:

"The Lord Himself will give you a sign. The virgin will be with child and will give birth to a son and will call him Immanuel"

and Micah 5:2:-

"But you Bethlehem Ehrathah, though you are small among the clans of Judah, out of you will come for me one who will be ruler over Israel, whose origins are from of old, from ancient times"...........

speak not only of the Messiah being born of a virgin, but also concerning the designation of his birthplace – Bethlehem of Judea. No Bible believer, indwelt by the Spirit of Christ (Messiah), would or could accept the emergence of the Messiah from any modern metropolis such as London, Los Angeles, New York or Miami!

Not once, not twice, but repeatedly, prophecies in the Old Testament (Hebrew word: Tenach), concerning Jesus, were literally fulfilled by, in and through His life on earth. Therefore, surely such prophecies concerning the nation, people and future of Israel should be afforded similar literal translation?

The proponents of Replacement Theology reject this exegesis when it comes to Israel and it, therefore, becomes a simple matter to 'spiritualize' or 'allegorize' literal truth. By doing this, the conclusion is made that the Church has replaced Israel in the purpose of God.

I have never met one disciple of this school of thought who has been able to explain away prophecy upon prophecy concerning the dispersion and re-gathering of the Jewish people.

In 2,000 years of Church history, it has certainly never been true of the Christian Church that she has ever been dispersed and then re-gathered again.

The past popularity of Replacement Theology and its universal 'success' is owing, not only to the allegorical method of interpretation applied by Christian and religious schools of thought, but by significant and historical facts which appear to justify this method of thinking.

Not the least of these facts is the notion that, as Israel rejected Jesus' claim to Divinity and Messiahship, so God would inevitably deal with Israel, punitively, by rejecting the nation and dispersing its people. It was a dispersion so immense, no observer over 1900 years could believe the Jews would ever again enter into the Promised Land.

For almost 2000 years, the fate of the 'wandering Jew' would appear to the world to justify the doctrinal position governing the adherents of Replacement Theology. If the term Replacement Theology was never used in the two millennia, or, for that matter, even understood, yet the fate of the Jews appear to support those who believed in Replacement Theology. That is, until 1948!

The suffering of the Jewish people can be traced back to earliest Biblical times, but in the Common Era (C.E. to the Jew; A.D. to the Gentile) it goes back to the first century. Israel as a nation has rarely known any relative peace. We can chart its history right back to the beginnings of the nation through the Patriarchs (Israel's 'Founding Fathers') Abraham, Isaac and Jacob.

In A.D. 70, the city of Jerusalem was desecrated by the Roman armies of Titus – the temple destroyed and the Jews forced into worldwide migration. The Roman persecution was so thorough it did not cease until the reign of Hadrian in A.D. 135. There was barely a Jew left in the land.

Simultaneously, the Christian Church was growing at an outstanding pace. However, what most Gentiles fail to realize is that the 'Church' of the first three centuries was primarily a 'Jewish Church'!

The body of Christ on earth at that time comprised mostly Jewish believers in a Jewish Messiah. The early believers engaged in Jewish culture, enjoyed the Jewish feasts but related Yom Kippur (The Jewish holiday of the Day of Atonement)[10] to the death of Yeshua upon a Jerusalem cross. His death was a complete, finished and sufficient sacrifice for their sins and salvation.

---

[10] "Yom Kippur." .."the last of the 10 days of penitence which begins with Rosh Hashana – the Jewish New Year"...Oxford Dictionary...2nd Edition...1996..

Only after Constantine's decree that the entire Roman Empire be 'christian', and his simultaneous persecution of Jews, did the separation occur between Christianity and Judaism. This period of time witnessed the beginning of the pendulum swinging from a Church comprising mostly Jewish believers in Jesus, into a Church beginning to infuse with Gentiles.

It was not long before Jewish belief in the Messiahship of Jesus began to wane as they suffered persecution under Constantine. Very soon, any understanding of 'The Day of Atonement' being related to the finished work of salvation through Jesus death upon the Cross, regressed back to their understanding of only the Tenach (the Old Testament). The 'Day of Atonement' became once again, an entrenched legalistic, religious, tradition!

When God 'performs' on the earth, He never does so simply to achieve only one purpose. Often unbeknown to our limited, finite, understanding is the truth He is doing a whole range of things at any one time, with a whole bunch of His children! And with a whole bunch who are not!

It is called 'believing in an Absolute, Sovereign God'. Most western Christians pay lip service to this, but fall short in the practical outworking of this truth into their daily lives.

The migration and dispersion of the Jews from Israel in the first two centuries A.D. included many Jewish believers in Yeshua (Jesus). Some were by compulsion, some by choice. Not least, in both groups, were some of Jesus' original 12 disciples and their disciples also.

In other words, it was these Jewish believers who first spread the tentacles of the Gospel in missionary enterprise throughout the then known world. This was the glad, good news. But, this was also the sad bad news! From those days until now, the Gentile converts to the Faith (and particularly their church leaders) have espoused Replacement Theology doctrine.

Jewish people were no longer becoming believers in Jesus. The emperor not only castigated ALL Jewish people but his goal was nothing less than complete and utter genocide!

Intrinsic in this belief of the so-called christians was the removal of the People called 'Israelites'. Israel, the nation, had previously been removed when Rome changed its name to Palestine. It did so partially from a taunting desire to demonize the Jewish nation by creating a name as closely akin as possible to that of Israel's implacable enemies - the Philistines. Philistine/Palestine - it worked.

The vast majority of Christendom now believed God transferred to the Church all the rights and privileges once bestowed upon the nation of Israel. The Jews no longer held any place of importance in God's plan for the world.

The tragedy of this is, the TRUTH lies in exact opposition to this!

Rather than Jewish suffering being the *cause* of Replacement Theology (i.e. God punishing Israel for its rejection of His Son), it is in fact the *consequence* of Replace-ment Theology.

The wandering Jew is now dispersed to the four corners of the globe and assimilated into whatever nation and ethnic community he finds himself.

Only the vague ritual toast at every Passover ("Next year in Jerusalem") kept the flame of hope flickering for a return to Israel. The early Church leaders like Origen unwittingly pioneered an anti-Semitic program which has stretched over 2,000 years. Evermore sadly, it continues in the 21st century - more vociferous and violent than ever!

CHAPTER 3

THE IMPACT OF REPLACEMENT THEOLOGY UPON HISTORY

—⚏—

The real truth is, if Replacement Theology had not taken such a hold upon the Christian Church in its infancy, much of the hatred, persecution and atrocities, perpetrated against the Jews worldwide, would never have occurred. At least not on the scale history has recorded. However, since the beginning of time, and, indeed, even in eternity itself, the warfare between God and Lucifer has continued. The sin of Adam and Eve simply transferred the theatre of war to planet earth. Replacement Theology merely became a dispensational weapon in the hands of God's archenemy. As Christians, we believe the Word of God clearly teaches Lucifer (Satan) had a demonically, inspired plan and purpose to destroy Jesus' descendants after the flesh. It was a plan in operation before the birth of the Messiah, and it is a plan still in operation over 2,000 years after His birth.

There is no question about it. In the embryonic days of the Church, Jews were indeed responsible for persecution of those who preferred to follow Jesus the Nazarene. Yes, Jewish Jews persecuted their fellow countrymen who became

"Christian" Jews. Today the latter are known as "Messianic Jews." One of the saddest facts about God's ancient chosen people is that this line of distinction and division still remains. Not only is it the present situation in Israel, but also in the world, wherever Jewish people become believers in Yeshua (Jesus), the Jewish Messiah.

Three centuries had hardly passed in the Common Era (C.E. or A.D.), and there is a reversal in behaviour. No longer are Christians being oppressed by Jews. Both Jews and genuine Christians together are being persecuted by those who only call themselves "christian."

From the mid-4th century, the Roman Empire had adopted "institutionalized Christianity." But it was a "Christianity" in name only. History declares it was Constantine's reign which inaugurated hatred and mass murder against BOTH peoples of the Book - Jew and Christian.

It remains a sad fact that anti-Christian forces amongst Jewish people today act in persecution and oppression simply because of their failure to understand the difference between "christian" and Christian!

They also have historically equated "Gentile" with "Christian." Therefore amongst the more radical elements of Orthodox Judaism there exists still a resentment of anyone NOT Jewish, and their vicious hatred is reserved for Christian and Messianic Jew alike who dare approach Jewish people with the Gospel of Jesus Christ.

YET, I believe it behoves those of us who claim to love the Jewish Messiah to demonstrate a spirit of compassion and love for these spiritually blind "relatives" of Yeshua (Jesus). Paul exhorts us to do this in his letter to the Romans. History likewise compels us when we consider what this race has suffered at the hands of those who have professed the name of Christianity.

When I first visited Israel 30 years ago, there was one tiny, fledgling, Messianic Fellowship emerging in the Galilee town of Tiberias. Today there are over 130 such Congregations throughout Israel. It is a miracle of God's Grace.

The universal declaration by the Emperor Constantine that Christianity become the acceptable orthodox religion of the Roman Empire was accompanied by an equally strong conviction of his intolerance toward Jews and Judaism. His "paganized universal church" – the fulfillment of his lifelong dream –offered no accommodation whatsoever for a Jew - regardless whether an individual Jew by race did or did not believe in the Jewish Messiah, Yeshua (Jesus).

Not only did Constantine view Judaism as falling radically short in its non-acceptance of Jesus' Messiahship, he also held it, and its adherents, as being fully responsible for the death of Jesus. Persecution against the Jewish people was seen to be the barometer of spiritual maturity and clear evidence of a "christian's" devotion to Jesus! It's somewhat bizarre logic centralized on what the proponents of Replacement Theology believed the greatest crime ever committed by humanity – the crime of Deicide! In essence, they accused the Jews of the murder of God Himself!

This most heinous act was seen by the Christian Church to be the sole responsibility and accountability of the race of people known as Jews. In the eyes of these professing loyalists of Jesus, it became a matter of logic to treat the murderers of their Redeemer with absolute contempt, disdain and even abject hatred – thus demonstrating their deepest devotion to the Galilean miracle-worker!

From the earliest writings of the Christian Church's leadership (historically referred to as "the Early Church Fathers"), was spewed out the most violent anti-Semitic rhetoric. The inexorable vitriol of this language did not relent from the early Church era through to the 11th and 12th centuries. Ask most professing Christians today to identify and esteem the period of the Crusades to Palestine, and you will hear lauded their praise and endorsement of such "valiant and zealous men of faith!"

What a tragedy in history that the militaristic zeal of these "religious" pilgrims (identified by the cross symbolically emblazoned on each Crusader's shield) did not embrace a similar devotion to Jesus by respecting and loving those who were His descendants by race?

In fact, such was their hatred of the Jews, they thought nothing of burning whole synagogues filled with Jewish worshippers. The unquenchable thirst to maim and kill in the name of Christ would not be assuaged in over a century. During that period, the 300,000 Jewish inhabitants in the Holy Land decreased to a figure a little more than a thousand.

As the time-clock moves forward a further 600 years, we arrive at an era in Church history which proves to be monumental in the annals of Christendom. It was the "Reformation Period."

The 16th century Reformation produced amazing writings from the pens of the spiritual colossus of Christian teachers and writers. They were men who saw through the corruption, hypocrisy and heresy promulgated by the Vatican in Rome. Many of them had been raised and educated by the Roman Catholic Church.

At some point in their journey of life, they heard the true pure Gospel of Grace preached, taught, lived or read. They were men, women and children who, in their day, were the "light of the world" and "the salt of the earth" for the Kingdom of God. Their names were written indelibly in the Lamb's Book of Life.

The Reformers are those whose legacy has come down to us through the miraculous preservation of the printed word; books such as, Fox's Book of Martyrs, recording the accounts of a multitude of ignominious deaths of the saints. Ignominious because it was unthinkable for 'professing' Christians (Roman Catholics) to wilfully murder fellow

Christians (non-Roman Catholics). Not only was it the deaths of these martyrs, it was the manner of their deaths. The executions of these people were reprehensible. The testimonies of these martyrs - glorious!

This remnant of non-Roman Catholics, through their lives and deaths, protested against both Church and State. They became 'Protestants', and thus began the 'Protestant Reformation'. It was a golden era for the true Church of Christ. But, it was an era tarnished.......stained with the blood of Jewish people.

Probably the most popularized of the leaders of the Reformation in Germany was a young Catholic priest by the name of Martin Luther.

I have previously mentioned that Luther, by reading the book of Romans in the Bible, discovered the liberating truth of 'justification by faith'. That is, contrary to the emphasis of the Catholic Church, whose teaching was a salvation based upon religious works, deeds, penances, and adherence to laws and traditions, Luther took the plain, simple, literal script of the Bible.

He applied the dictum that the only way to understand Scripture, is to compare Scripture with Scripture, and allow God's own Holy Spirit to illuminate the heart, and enable the recipient to grasp the truth about God's grace in Christ!

For Luther, this personal salvation was both miraculous and liberating. The remarkable change in the life and teaching of a simple Roman Catholic priest challenged the establishment of Rome as never before. Luther's new birth changed the entire course of Church history.

However, to Luther, such a revelation of Christ caused him to believe that multitudes of Jewish people worldwide would now swarm into membership of the Christian Church. It did not happen.

It was an incomprehensible shock to Luther, and, later in his life, the enormity of his reaction to this, began to show itself in a dark side. Not only did Luther resent Jewish unbelief, but also there grew within him a bitter hatred toward this people. The tragedy of Martin Luther is that, before his death, he became an avowed anti-Semite! He wrote a book in the latter part of his life, entitled On the Jews and their Lies. He certainly lost his 'hero status' with this writer on my discovery of this fact. How tragic for the world!

You may ask, "Why?"

Adolf Hitler chose this particular dogma of Luther's upon which to base his own philosophy of life and politics. Hitler in his classic autobiography, Mein Kampf, writes of Luther's anti-Semitism, and lauds the major contribution and influence of Luther's work upon his own dastardly 'Final Solution of the Jewish Problem'. In fact Hitler went so far as to declare, "I have done to the Jews what the Lord told me to do!"

If Hitler had only responded to Luther's personal discovery of Paul's teaching in his letter to the Christians in Rome, that, "a man is justified by faith and not by works of the law" (Romans 3:28), indubitably, the history books would have been otherwise written. It is one of the greatest oxymorons in the history of the Church. Luther, this Roman Catholic priest-cum-hero of the Reformation, who received such a profound, transforming revelation that the Divine Scriptures should be accepted literally, is both at one, and the same time, persuaded to vilify the Jewish people.

Such was the demonic hold upon this theological colossus, he found himself in the closing act of his life writing a book entitled Against Jews and Their Lies. Luther's spoken and written contempt for the sons of Israel by race, tragically became a 'mythical textbook' around which the infamous Hitler and his evil Nazi philosophy built the constitution for the Third Reich four centuries later.

Hitler saw no discrepancy between Germany's Catholic and Lutheran theology and, simultaneously, holding an intense hatred of Judaism and Jews – even if they were German Jews! It was precisely Luther's legacy of hate which became the logic of Nazism.

Certainly through the centuries, the world's treatment of the Jew, whether by followers of Islam or Christianity, would seemingly place history supporting those who espoused and promulgated Replacement Theology.

Surely, the overwhelming evidence of the long-suffering of the Jewish people must demonstrate God's rejection of them and, therefore, justify His punishment upon them? At least, this was the prevalent thinking of the Gentile world in Luther's Day. Subtly and not so subtly, such thinking still prevails.

Has any ethnic group of people suffered as this race has? In the early 1940's, two-thirds of the entire race on the planet were exterminated. Now, half a century later, and the world's political and diplomatic sounding-board, the United Nations, is advocating the surrender of Jewish land.

The Islamic nations, holding the trump card called OIL, influence the game, and find extreme consolation in being able to hide behind the apron of the U.N.

What will be left of the "wandering Jews" - worldwide "Israel"? What will be left of the Land and nation of Israel?

Surely, the God of Abraham, Isaac and Jacob has been "replacing" them with this mystical, invisible, organization called the "Christian Church"?

Surely the rightful owners of the Land must be Palestinians? Surely God is a God of justice? He could not possibly justify Israel's presence in a land called Palestine?

Surely God cannot endorse Israel going into Lebanon seeking to root out Hezbollah terrorists?

Surely, surely, surely?

It is not the mandate for this book to discuss the politics of the Middle East. Nor is it to discuss the intricacies of Islam and its frightening growth in our world. It is also not a cop out on my part in avoiding these. To discuss them would simply deviate from the burden of my heart, hopefully to enlighten you, the reader, on the past and present impact of Replacement Theology upon:

1. *the Church*
2. *Israel and the Jewish People*
3. *the world*

Readers who know of my ministry through MENORAH will be cognizant of the fact that I love to teach the truth of God's Word on this subject.

It IS the purpose of this book, however, to declare that, rather than being the result of this tragic history, Replacement Theology is, in fact, the cause of it. I also maintain that Jewish history, rather than denying Israel her place among the nations, actually affirms God's unconditional choice of Israel as His chosen people by divine covenant.

The very existence, survival and revival of the fortunes of God's ancient people are an argument against Replacement Theology and NOT an argument for it.

The fact that such a nation called Israel is printed in the most recently published map of the world today, is nothing short of a divine miracle. (Only maps published by Islamic companies do NOT include Israel). Until 1948 there was not a map in the world with Israel printed on it!

No nation in history has been dispersed twice from its own land, and twice returned. It has happened to NO other nation in history.

No nation has ever lost its language (which is a country's national identity), only to have it restored and revived after 2000 years. It has happened to NO other nation.

It is nothing short of a divine act this people has survived over three millennia of persecution, assimilation and attempted genocide – yet has remained a nation amongst nations. Its military might is ranked amongst the strongest five powers in the world. Not bad for a country no larger than Wales, the State of New Jersey, or Canada's Vancouver Island!

Many are the passages of Scripture which speak of the indestructibility of the Jewish people. One of these is Malachi 3:6, which speaks of the sovereignty of God, the unchangeableness of His nature and the permanency of the Sons of Jacob, "I the Lord do not change so you, descendants of Jacob (Israel) are not destroyed."

This has to be the answer to those holding tenaciously to the teaching known as Replacement Theology and who argue that Israel has been replaced by the Church.

CHAPTER 4

DOES ISRAEL HAVE ANY RIGHT WITH RESPECT TO 'THE LAND?'

—m—

When we come to the issue of "The Holy Land," the question is continually asked by the secular media, "What rights does Israel have with respect to the land, for centuries known as Palestine?"

Arguments for, but mostly against, are batted back and forth by people across the world. As I write these words, Israel has recently experienced its seventh war since the formation of its modern statehood in 1948. Public opinion in Gallup polls have never been so divided over the question of Israel's rights.

Surely, there is a more basic question requiring an answer – "Who has the ultimate AUTHORITY to determine what rights, if any, Israel has to the land?"

The Judaeo-Christian believer, believing in the Bible as God's divine authority for faith and practice in the world, will conclude that God alone determines the "rights" any of us has.

I will go further and declare that, a true disciple of Jesus Christ, in comprehending Biblical teaching concerning the universal nature of the sin principle, believes and accepts that no human being has any 'rights' before a just and holy God. Everything I have, or own, is by virtue of the grace and mercy of God alone!

The genuine Christian believer holds to a position which declares human reasoning or feeling not to be authoritative. Rather, a thing is right or wrong by virtue of divine decree.

As someone once wrote, "Morality exists because God exists. Authority exists because God exists."

David Hocking in his superb booklet entitled *What the Bible Says About Israel and its Land*, declares Israel's history as being "bathed in divine authority and direction."[11] There are over 3,000 references to Israel in the Bible; only a very ignorant student of the Word of God would conclude God to be a passive observer to all that occurs in the land of Israel. He has in fact already destined the 'rights' of the Jewish people to their own land.

In Deuteronomy 11:12, he says to the nation, "The eyes of the Lord your God are always on it, from the beginning even to the end of the year."

Prior to 1948, the concept of a teaching in Scripture declaring the coming of Jesus Christ into the world thus making Israel obsolete, was not only plausible to the Christian world, it was also tenable. It simply was not known as Replacement Theology.

Rome's tyrannical monopoly in the Middle East saw to it that the larger portion of Israel's entire population was dispersed to the four corners of the globe by A.D. 135. It was not until the last two decades of the 19th century was there so much as a glimmer on the horizon of any re-gathering of the legitimate Sons of Abraham.

---

[11] Hocking, David, *What the Bible Says About Israel and its Land*, Published by..Calvary Communications Inc...Multnomah Press,Portland, Oregon,97266...1983..

In 586 B.C. the nation was taken into captivity by its conquerors – the Babylonians (present day Iraq). The Bible books of Ezra and, particularly, Nehemiah, narrate for us the wonder of Israel's first return to the land in the 4th century BC. What had amazingly transpired in that return would most certainly never happen again. For dispersion and subsequent return to occur a second time in her history would be, for Israel, nothing short of miraculous. It would be for *any* nation.

However, it is precisely the business of the miraculous in which God excels – it is in His nature. This Biblical truth is especially applicable when it relates to His "Chosen People."

At the end of World War II, with one-third of world Jewry lying on the ash heaps of Polish and German soil, resurrection life entered into the hearts of many European Jewish men, women and children. These were, arguably, deemed 'blessed' to still be alive. 'Arguably' because multitudes had lost family members at the hands of the despicable atrocities committed by the Nazis and, especially, the SS. Many had lost all hope for living.

Only the flickering vision of the unifying cry, "Next Year in Jerusalem" (watchword of the "wandering Jew" for centuries) kept their hopes alive.

A post-war Germany is now divided into two. Jews finding themselves in Western Germany were free - free to travel - free to go 'home' to what was then Palestine - i.e. if the British would allow them access.

Jews entrenched east of the Berlin Wall found themselves in captivity yet again, this time to a new oppressor – the communist regime of the Soviet Union. Many East German Jews at the end of World War Two viewed their lives as passing from ownership by one 'master race' (Nazism), to ownership by another (Soviet Communism).

It looks as if they, and their seed, would never get anywhere near the Mediterranean port of Haifa.

But the heart of the Jew has always been inspired by hope. This is why the name of Israel's national anthem is "Ha Tikvah" – the Hope.

God's multiple Biblical promises to them in the Old Testament Scriptures (the Tenach) was for the possession in perpetuity of the Land of Canaan – FOREVER.

When we speak of 'the Land' we are touching the jugular of the Middle East 'problem' (so-called). At least, subsequent to May 14, 1948, the politicians and media consistently referred to it as a 'problem'. One does not have to be a student of the Middle East today to be aware that nothing has really changed.

This writer, in company with multitudes of Judaeo-Christian believers worldwide, does not accept the limitations and restrictions imposed upon Israel by the United Nations with respect to 'the Land'.

What gives any nation, or body of nations, any authority to deny Holy Scripture, and reject the words of God Himself, especially with respect to the divinely appointed inheritance granted Israel and her people?

What 'right' has any mere created human being, or organization of human beings, to establish a 'kingdom of man', and name it 'the United Nations'?

Any thinking observer of the United Nations and its procedural strategy cannot but be cognizant of one very simple fact – the nations of the 21st century are far from being 'united'! Forgive me for one trite comment, but its initials are more apropos 'United Nothing' - at least it is as far as it's dealings with Israel are concerned.

Here is where the Kingdom of God and the kingdom of this world, part company. As we enter into a new millennium, the words of the late 20th century writer, theologian and prophet, Francis Schaeffer, appear to be verified as truth:

"The watershed of the next generation will be the question of the authority and divine inspiration of the Bible." For the true Christian believer, this is the acid test in his or her devotion to Christ.

The Apostle Peter, in I Peter 3:15, exhorts the Christian to, "Give a reason for the hope within you."

As the Christians, "tikvah" (hope) is in the words, deeds and cross of the Jewish Messiah; likewise the Jewish tikvah is in the same, "For there is neither Jew nor Greek...you are all one in Christ Jesus." (Galatians 3:28) To the earthly seed of Abraham (Israel), He promised 'the Land'. To the heavenly seed of Abraham (the Church) He promised 'eternal life'.

Israel's 'rights' to 'the land' are circumvented only by the words of God. Those words of promise and hope merely BEGIN in the first book of the Bible - "The Lord made a covenant with Abram saying, 'To your descendants I have given this land, from the river of Egypt, as far as the great river, the river Euphrates.'" (Genesis 15:18)

An inability or unwillingness to perceive, discern, comprehend or believe this, might simply have something to do with the observation made upon our present western world by the aforementioned Francis Schaeffer: "At the end of the 20th century we will be witnessing in Europe and North America what we can only describe as a 'post-Christian society.'"

In one of God's earliest references to 'the Land', God actually gives Moses a delineated, dimensional outline with respect to its borders. In the Book of Numbers 34:1-15 are to be found fascinating details affecting a number of territorial issues hotly disputed today by the enemies of Israel. Issues, which when based upon a belief in and acceptance of God's authority over His world and His Word, would resound firmly in favour of Israel being Israel.

It is neither cowardice nor evasion on my part, but it is not within the scope of the book's subject for this writer to elaborate on this. I would refer the reader to the brilliant book, Philistine: The Great Deception, by the New Zealand writer, Ramon Bennett. A 'must read' for anyone whose appetite for truth, hopefully, I have whetted.

However, based solely upon the Word of God itself and alone, I offer certain Biblical facts totally supporting Israel's right to the Land. When we speak of 'Israel', we speak uniquely, solely and exclusively of 'the Jewish people':

1. It is God's land, not man's - and as such belongs to Him.

2. The land was not earned or bought – rather it was a gift given by God to the descendants of Abraham.

   "Then the Lord appeared to Abram and said, 'To your descendants I will give this land.' And there he built an altar to the Lord, who had appeared to him." (Genesis 12:7)

   "For all the land that you see I give to you and your descendants forever." (Genesis 13:15)

   "On the same day the Lord made a covenant with Abram, saying: To your descendants I have given this land, from the river of Egypt to the great river, the River Euphrates." (Genesis 15:18)

3. God's historical and chronological dealings with Israel were always on the basis of an 'unconditional covenant' – this gift of Land was no different.

   "I will establish my covenant as an everlasting covenant between me and you and your descendants after you for the generations to come, by your God and the God of your descendants after you. The whole land of Canaan, where you are now an alien, I will give as an everlasting possession to you and your descendants after you; and I will be your God." (Genesis 17:7-8)

"If his sons forsake my law and do not follow my statutes, if they violate my decrees and fail to keep my commands, I will punish their sin with the rod, their iniquity with flogging; but I will not take my love from him, nor will I ever betray my faithfulness. I will not violate my covenant or alter what my lips have uttered. Once for all, I have sworn by my holiness – and I will not lie to David – that his line will continue forever and his throne endures before me like the sun; it will be established forever like the moon, the faithful witness in the sky." (Psalm 89:30-37)

"The Lord did not set his affection on you and choose you because you were more numerous than other peoples, for you were the fewest of all peoples. But it was because the Lord loved you and kept the oath he swore to your forefathers that he brought you out with a mighty hand and redeemed you from the land of slavery, from the power of Pharaoh King of Egypt. Know therefore that the Lord your God is God; he is the faithful God, keeping his covenant of love to a thousand generations of those who love him and keep his commands." (Deuteronomy 7:7-9)

4. Contrary to the belief of many people, God does declare He will bless Abraham's illegitimate son, Ishmael. BUT He enters into a Covenant with the true

son, Isaac. HERE is the origin of what is commonly referred to as the "Middle East Problem."

"As for Ishmael, I will surely bless him; I will make him fruitful and will greatly increase his numbers. He will be the father of twelve rulers, and I will make him into a great nation. BUT My Covenant I will establish with Isaac." (Genesis 17:20-21)

"Even God had said to him, 'It is through Isaac that your offspring will be reckoned.'" (Hebrews 11:18)

5. This gift was not given to the other legitimate sons of Abraham -.ONLY to Isaac!

"Abraham left everything he owned to Isaac. But while he was still living, he gave gifts to the sons of his concubines and sent them away from his son Isaac to the land of the east." (Genesis 25:5-6)

"Stay in this land for a while, and I will be with you and will bless you. For to you and your descendants I will give all these lands and will confirm the oath I swore to your father Abraham." (Genesis 26:3)

6. This land was not gifted to the descendants of Esau, but only to those of Jacob.

"Not only that, but Rebekah's children had one and the same father, our father Isaac. Yet, before the twins were born or had done anything good or bad – in order that God's purpose in election might stand: not by works but by him who calls – she was told, 'The older will serve the younger.' Just as it is written: 'Jacob I loved, but Esau I hated.'" (Note: in man's fallible humanness, he questions how it is possible for a 'loving God' to 'hate Esau', but somehow never asks how a just, righteous and holy God could possibly love a wretch like Jacob!) (Romans 9:10-13)

"May he give you and your descendants the blessing given to Abraham, so that you may take possession of the land where you now live as an alien, the land God gave to Abraham." (Genesis 28:4)

"Jacob left Beersheba and set out for Haran. When he reached a certain place, he stopped for the night because the sun had set. Taking one of the stones there, he put it under his head and lay down to sleep. He had a dream in which he saw a stairway resting on the earth, with its top reaching to heaven, and the angels of God were ascending and descending on it. There above it stood the Lord, and he said, 'I am the Lord, the God of your father Abraham and the God of Isaac. I will give you and your descendants the land on which you are lying. Your descendants will be like the dust of the earth, and you will spread out to the west and to the east, to the north and to the south. All peoples on earth will be blessed through you and your offspring. I am with you and will watch over you wherever you go, and I will bring you back to this land. I will not leave you until I have done what I have promised you.' When Jacob awoke from his sleep, he thought, 'Surely the Lord is in this place, and I was not aware of it.' He was afraid and said, 'How awesome is this place! This is none other

than the house of God; this is the gate of heaven.'"
(Genesis 28:10-17)

"After Jacob returned from Paddan Aram, God
appeared to him again and bless him. God said to
him, 'Your name is Jacob, but you will no longer
be called Jacob; your name will be Israel.' So he
named him Israel. And God said to him, 'I am God
Almighty; be fruitful and increase in number. A
nation and a community of nations will come from
you, and kings will come from your body. The land
I gave to Abraham and Isaac I also give to you, and
I will give this land to your descendants after you.'
Then God went up from him at the place where he
had talked with him. Jacob set up a stone pillar at the
place where God had talked with him, and he poured
out a drink offering on it; he also poured oil on it.
Jacob called the place where God had talked with
him Bethel." (Genesis 35:9-15)

"Esau took his wives and sons and daughters and
all the members of his household, as well as his livestock and all his other animals and all the goods he
had acquired in Canaan, and moved to a land some
distance from his brother Jacob. Their possessions
were too great for them to remain together; the land
where they were staying could not support them both
because of their livestock. So Esau (that is, Edom)
settled in the hill country of Seir. This is the account
of Esau the father of the Edomites in the hill country
of Seir." (Genesis 36:6-9)

"I will go down to Egypt with you, and I will
surely bring you back again. And Joseph's own hand
will close your eyes." (Genesis 46:4)

"Jacob said to Joseph, 'God Almighty appeared to me at Luz in the land of Canaan, and there be blessed me and said to me, "I am going to make you fruitful and will increase your numbers. I will make you a community of peoples, and I will give this land as an everlasting possession to your descendants after you."'" (Genesis 48:3-4)

"Then Joseph said to his brothers, 'I am about to die. But God will surely come to your aid and take you up out of this land to the land he promised on oath to Abraham, Isaac and Jacob.'" (Genesis 50:24)

7. During the years of bondage in Egypt and the wilderness wanderings, God continued to remind Israel of this covenant.

"God heard their groaning and he remembered his covenant with Abraham, with Isaac and with Jacob." (Exodus 2:24)

"So I have come down to rescue them from the hand of the Egyptians and to bring them up out of that land into a good and spacious land, a land flowing with milk and honey – the home of the Canaanites, Hittites, Amorites, Perizzites, Hivites and Jebusites." (Exodus 3:8)

"God also said to Moses, 'Say to the Israelites, "The Lord, the God of your fathers – the God of Abraham, the God of Isaac and the God of Jacob – has sent me to you." This is my name forever, the name by which I am to be remembered from generation to generation. "Go, assemble the elders of Israel and say to them, 'The Lord, the God of your fathers

– the God of Abraham, Isaac and Jacob – appeared to me and said: I have watched over you and have seen what has been done to you in Egypt. And I have promised to bring you up out of your misery in Egypt into the land of the Canaanites, Hittites, Amorites, Perizzites, Hivites and Jebusites – a land flowing with milk and honey.'"" (Exodus 3:15-17)

"The Lord said to Moses, 'Now you will see what I will do to Pharaoh: Because of my mighty hand he will let them go; because of my mighty hand he will drive them out of his country.' God also said to Moses, 'I am the Lord. I appeared to Abraham, to Isaac and to Jacob as God Almighty, but by my name the Lord I did not make myself known to them. I also established my covenant with them to give them the land of Canaan, where they lived as aliens. Moreover, I have heard the groaning of the Israelites, whom the Egyptians are enslaving, and I have remembered my covenant. Therefore, say to the Israelites, "I am the Lord, and I will bring you out from under the yoke of the Egyptians. I will free you from being slaves to them, and I will redeem you with an outstretched arm and with mighty acts of judgment. I will take you as my own people, and I will be your God. Then you will know that I am the Lord your God, who brought you out from under the yoke of the Egyptians. And I will bring you to the land I swore with uplifted hand to give to Abraham, to Isaac and to Jacob. I will give it to you as a possession. I am the Lord."'" (Exodus 6:1-8)

"When the Lord brings you into the land of the Canaanites, Hittites, Amorites, Hivites and Jebusites – the land he swore to your forefathers to give you, a land flowing with milk and honey – you are to observe this ceremony in this month." (Exodus 13:5)

"You will bring them in and plant them on the mountain of your inheritance – the place, O Lord, you made for your dwelling, the sanctuary, O Lord, your hands established." (Exodus 15:17)

"Remember your servants Abraham, Isaac and Israel, to whom you swore by your own self; 'I will make your descendants as numerous as the stars in the sky and I will give your descendants all this land I promised them, and it will be their inheritance forever.'" (Exodus 32:13)

"But I said to you, 'You will possess their land; I will give it to you as an inheritance, a land flowing with milk and honey.' I am the Lord your God, who has set you apart from the nations." (Leviticus 20:24)

"I am the Lord your God, who brought you out of Egypt to give you the land of Canaan and to be your God." (Leviticus 25:38)

8. The command of God is that Israel should conquer the land He had given them.

"See, I have given you this land. Go in and take possession of the land that the Lord swore he would give to your fathers – to Abraham, Isaac and Jacob – and to their descendants after them." (Deuteronomy 1:8)

"Go up to the top of Pisgah and look west and north and south and east. Look at the land with your own eyes, since you are not going to cross this Jordan. But commission Joshua, and encourage and strengthen him, for he will lead this people across and will cause them to inherit the land that you will see." (Deuteronomy 3:27-28)

"But be assured today that the Lord your God is the one who goes across ahead of you like a devouring fire. He will destroy them; he will subdue them before you. And you will drive them out and annihilate them quickly, as the Lord has promised you. After the Lord your God has driven them out before you, do not say to yourself, 'The Lord has brought me here to take possession of this land because of my righteousness.' No, it is on account of the wickedness of these nations that the Lord is going to drive them out before you. It is not because of your righteousness or your integrity that you are going in to take possession of their land; but on account of the wickedness of these nations, the Lord your God will drive them out before you, to accomplish what he swore to your fathers, to Abraham, Isaac and Jacob." (Deuteronomy 9:3-5)

9. The sons and subsequent captivities of Israel did not change or alter their divine right to the land.

"But if they will confess their sins and the sins of their fathers – their treachery against me and their hostility toward me, which made me hostile toward them so that I sent them into the land of their enemies – then when their uncircumcised hearts are humbled and they pay for their sin, I will remember my cove-

nant with Jacob and my covenant with Isaac and my
covenant with Abraham, and I will remember the land.
For the land will be deserted by them and will enjoy
its Sabbaths while it lies desolate without them. They
will pay for their sins because they rejected my laws
and abhorred my decrees. Yet in spite of this, when
they are in the land of their enemies, I will not reject
them or abhor them so as to destroy them completely,
breaking my covenant with them. I am the Lord their
God. But for their sake I will remember the covenant
with their ancestors whom I brought out of Egypt
in the sight of the nations to be their God. I am the
Lord." (Leviticus 26:40-45)

"When all these blessings and curses I have set
before you come upon you and you take them to heart
wherever the Lord your God disperses you among
the nations, and when you and your children return
to the Lord your God and obey him with all your
heart and with all your soul according to everything
I command you today, then the Lord your God will
restore your fortunes and have compassion on you
and gather you again from all the nations where he
scattered you. Even if you have been banished to the
most distant land under the heavens, from there the
Lord your God will gather you and bring you back.
He will bring you to the land that belonged to your
fathers, and you will take possession of it. He will
make you more prosperous and numerous than your
fathers." (Deuteronomy 30:1-5)

"Do not be afraid, for I am with you; I will bring
your children from the east and gather you from the
west. I will say to the north, 'Give them up!' and to
the south, 'Do not hold them back.' Bring my sons

from afar and my daughters from the ends of the earth – everyone who is called by my name, whom I created for my glory, whom I formed and made." (Isaiah 43:5-7)

"But they will say, 'As surely as the Lord lives, who brought the Israelites up out of the land of the north and out of all the countries where he had banished them.' For I will restore them to the land I gave their forefathers." (Jeremiah 16:15)

"Hear the word of the Lord, O nations; proclaim it in distant coastlands: He who scattered Israel will gather them and will watch over his flock like a shepherd." (Jeremiah 31:10)

"'I will bring back my exiled people Israel; they will rebuild the ruined cities and live in them. They will plant vineyards and drink their wine; they will make gardens and eat their fruit. I will plant Israel in their own land, never again to be uprooted from the land I have given them,' says the Lord your God." (Amos 9:14-15)

10. God's promise to Israel is as certain as the existence and order of the universe.

"This is what the Lord says, he who appoints the sun to shine by day; who decrees the moon and stars to shine by night, who stirs up the sea so that its waves roar – the Lord Almighty is his name: 'Only if these decrees vanish from my sight,' declares the Lord, 'will the descendants of Israel ever cease to be a nation before me.' This is what the Lord says: 'Only if the heavens above can be measured and the

foundations of the earth below be searched out will I
reject all the descendants of Israel because of all they
have done,' declares the Lord." (Jeremiah 31:35-37)

11. The name of this land is NOT Palestine – it never
was! The name of the land is ISRAEL. The Israeli
prophet Ezekiel, 2500 years ago spoke of the "last
days" (the end of time). He spoke of the restoration
both of this land, and the restoration of the Jewish
people to this land.

> "Then he said to me: 'Son of man, these bones
> are the whole house of Israel. They say, "Our bones
> are dried up and our hope is gone; we are cut off."
> Therefore prophesy and say to them, 'This is what
> the Sovereign Lord says: O my people, I am going to
> open your graves and bring you up from them; I will
> bring you back to the land of Israel.'" (not Palestine.)
> (Ezekiel 37:11-12)

> Ezekiel spoke of this as being a "miracle of God!"
> So often called "the land of Canaan," in the last days
> it will be called "Israel."

12. A total and complete restoration of Israel to its Land,
with peace and security, must be the precursor to the
coming (return) of the Messiah (prophesied abun-
dantly in Scripture).

Over the last 40 years, multitudes of Bible-believing
Christians have discovered a fresh inexplicable, God-given
love, for Israel – its People and its Land.

How could this be when for centuries Jews have suffered
indescribable atrocities at the hands of people who called
themselves 'Christians'? Why would Gentile Christians want

to align themselves with a nation so vehemently opposed by the majority of governments and people?

There is only one plausible answer – it is because of the teaching of the Bible itself. In particular, the multiple passages which speak clearly of the coming (return) of the Jewish Messiah.

What, to the evangelical (Bible believing) Christian is a divine certainty – the return of Jesus Christ to earth – probably, for the Jew, finds its closest expression in the words of Jerusalem's legendary mayor, the late Teddy Kollek, "When the Messiah comes, I shall not be at all surprised if he turns out to be Jesus of Nazareth!"

CHAPTER 5

GOD'S CHARACTER AND SALVATION

—⟋⟍—

In the previous Chapter, I cited numerous passages of Scripture appertaining to God's unconditional promises to Israel.

It would be relatively easy and enjoyable for me to exegete these passages one by one. I desist from doing so for only one reason - knowing how easily my 'butterfly mind' loves to wander from the subject in hand! They were given to lend solid Biblical evidence to the subject, and not in any way to become subjects in themselves.

The writer makes no apology for giving the reader so many! I am certain that the majority of my readers are Bible-believing people. If ever there was a time in history when we desperately need to hear God's Voice above all others, surely it is at the beginning of this new millennium?

If all these Scriptures are applied literally, not allegorically, and if we believe these promises can only be applied to the Jewish people, then the questions must surely be asked:

- How is it that Replacement Theology is still so rampant in our time?

- Why does the majority of Christendom still believe and accept its teaching?
- Why does the Church believe it has replaced Israel in the purpose of God?
- Why does the Church see herself as, 'The Israel of God'?

The Replacement Theology belief system asks a seemingly logical question: "How can a just God possibly contradict His own nature by restoring the Jewish people to their own Land?"

In the thinking of Replacement Theology adherents, the answer is simple: It is just not possible!

Our finite understanding of justice would tell us that, to the naked eye, this position appears logical and consistent with what we know of the justice of God.

Surely God could not, and would not, treat the 'murderers' of His Son in any other way, except the way of retribution?

Since Constantine's reign as Roman Emperor, certainly the Jews of the Diaspora[12] have not turned to Jesus of Nazareth in recognition of Him as their Messiah. At least, those resident in the land from A.D. 135 to A.D. 1948 certainly did not.

Even when the modern State of Israel was declared in May 1948, the majority of its political and military leadership were secular Zionists. They believed in the Jewish right to the 'Holy' Land, but did not relate being there to any word or deed of God. Two-thirds of present-day Israel is secular! Most Christians are ignorant of this truth.

Secular Zionism comprises as many belief systems as there are American Baptists : agnostics, secular Jews by race, carnal 'God-fearers', religious contradictions, and even atheists!

---

[12] The worldwide dispersion of the Jewish people from Israel under Roman Emperor Titus in A.D.70 and Harrian in A.D. 135.

For the enquiring reader who desires a deeper and wider knowledge of what is ostensibly referred to as Christian Zionism, there are a whole host of excellent books available. This ministry of MENORAH will be happy to assist in recommendations.

For the avid student seeking to understand the 'whys' and 'wherefores' of either Christian Zionism and/or Messianic Judaism, I must recommend Stan Telchin's expose in his book, Some Messianic Jews say, Messianic Judaism is NOT Christianity: A loving call to Unity.

It is certainly a mouthful of a title for a medium size book. However, Stan explores virtually every facet of Christian faith held by Jewish people today. In common with this writer he believes that, were it not for over 2,000 years of dastardly treatment meted out to ethnic Jews by 'professing christians', there would arguably be NO Messianic Judaism in our time.

I place the words 'professing Christians' in inverted commas for one very sound reason; simply speaking, a mere spoken word, or the professing of a Christian belief, does NOT necessarily imply or guarantee Christian behaviour!

What religious christians have perpetrated against the Jews over two centuries, in NO WAY reflects the behaviour modeled by Jesus for His disciples to emulate.

The Church's behaviour in this area has been anathema to that of Biblical Christianity espoused by Yeshua and Sha'ul (Jesus and Paul).

Some of the most gifted and eloquent preachers in the early Church were frighteningly infectious in their vitriolic diatribes against Jews. If it was merely a matter of rhetoric alone, the history books would read differently.

But it was not words alone. The deadly rhetoric led to two millennia of hate against the seed of Abraham, culminating in near genocide of the Jewish race.

One of the early Church Fathers (leaders) was Bishop John Chrysostom of Antioch. His unashamed 'Jew-bashing' rendered a series of eight sermons or homilies entitled, 'Against the Jews', in which he clearly denounced their race as the Christ-killers!

It was not only the congregations under John Chrysostom who were recipients of his obscene teachings but the multitude of priests in centuries to come, trained to revere and respect Chrysostom and his teachings.

Such was his virulent detestation of Jews, in his Eighth Homily he addressed the Christian members of his congregation who were medical patients of Jewish physicians: "Let me go so far as to say that even if they really do cure you, it is better to die than to run to God's enemies and be cured that way."

The Crusades of the Middle Ages began at the turn of the 12th century. Violence was a hallmark of their European travels, ostensibly known as pilgrimages.

Armed with a belief in Chrysostom's anti-Semitic doctrine, it propelled the Crusaders to rape, pillage and murder whole Jewish communities along Germany's Rhine River. They simply left Jewish bodies by the thousands in ditches and gullies, fodder for hungry wildlife.

For the God-fearing Jew of that day, theirs was a straight choice - apostasy or death. It is what the British call 'Hobson's Choice' - that is, in the situation there is absolutely NO choice at all! Most chose martyrdom.

Only the most ardent historians will note the year 1492 - Columbus' discovery of America. Yet, in that same year, the Edict of Expulsion was signed in Granada, Spain. Spanish Jews were given three choices: convert to Catholicism; leave the country; or, be burned at the stake. They were given 30 days to make their choice. This era was known as "the Spanish Inquisition".

170,000 Jews left the land to wander Europe on May 1, 1492.

Tens of thousands accepted baptism into the church of Rome. Outwardly they shed their Jewish identity, but in the privacy of their own homes they lived as Jews. These Jews became known as Marranos.

Fifty thousand were still eventually burned at the stake for heresy. This figure corresponds with the same number of U.S. and allied military lost in Vietnam, but then, who has ever heard of the Marranos?

The last Jew left Spain on July 31, 1492 and Pope Innocent III had 'triumphed'.

IF only the 'Spanish Inquisition' (as it became known) had finished there, but its aftermath and tributary repercussions of anti-Semitic hate swept through Europe for another 300 years.

From being one of THE heroic pioneers of the 1523 Protestant Reformation in Europe, it took only 20 years before Luther became a changed man. His utter frustration at the absence of Jewish interest in the Gospel spilt over into anger at their unwillingness to receive the message. It was not long before his anger turned to hate.

Hate spreads, and spread it did! Luther's influence on the Protestant world of the 16th, 17th and 18th centuries invoked scorn and derision upon the Jews. Many countries passed laws to segregate and punish Jews, based upon Luther's teachings, espoused in his book, Against Jews and their Lies.

It arguably led to the ultimate horror, the Holocaust (the Jewish term...Shoah)!

The term 'Messianic Judaism' was coined less than half a century ago, and, in Israel, came into use more emphatically since the miraculous victory of Israel in the 1973 Yom Kippur war.

The former President of the 'Voice of Hope' Radio Station, George Otis, recounts some of the miracles the Jewish military experienced in this war. It was a war Israel should 'never' have won in the 'natural'. Outnumbered and surprised, the nation was caught in synagogue or at home on the Jewish holiest day of the year, Yom Kippur - The Day of Atonement.

The Israelis were 'whipped' before they could touch their weapons.....that is, UNTIL God began to perform military and meteorological miracles of Biblical proportions. Within three weeks it was all over.....and the Syrian and Egyptian armies were decimated.

For a sabra[13] Jew to become 'Messianic' is almost tantamount to a Muslim disowning allegiance to Mohammed! The only difference is, Jews do not kill fellow Jews for converting outside of Judaism! They may feel like doing so, but to carry out such a deed would be unthinkable for a legitimate son of Abraham (hence the outrage amongst world-wide Jewry on the assassination of Prime Minister Yitzhak Rabin at the hands of a fellow Jew).

When I first visited Israel in 1977, there was only one Messianic Assembly in the country. Today there are known to be 130 or more as previously cited.. Their growth has been quite prolific since the Yom Kippur war of 1973 (not that there is necessarily any observed link between the two facts, apart from my earlier pronouncement).

Both the secular press, and Replacement Theology advocates in the religious media, delight to show the reader, "... what Jews in Israel are doing with the Palestinians."

In doing so, the religious media in particular, conclude there is no way the God of the Bible could acquiesce such injustice. The secular media dismisses any notion that any god could enter into the fray, and condemns Israel's deni-

---

[13] An Israeli Jew born IN the Land. A native-born Israeli Jew.

grating treatment of the Palestinians. To these people Israel has ignored the question of 'human rights' all together, and chosen for itself a path of isolation and self-destruction.

Politically and socially it is beyond question there have been injustices perpetrated, in the land, against the Palestinians. No Biblical conviction concerning the right of the Jewish people to live within the territory of Biblical Canaan absolve the Israeli government and military from living right, and acting righteously.

However, the historical evidence of the last 1700 years is indisputable. It has been the infrastructure of Replacement Theology which has propelled anti-Semitism in the non-Islamic world.

Together with radical, fundamentalist, Islam, Replacement Theology has fuelled the world's abhorrence for both the Jew, and Israel.

If God says, "I honour my Word above my Name," are we to agree with Him or disagree? If we agree, then every single inscripturated word relating His unconditional love and mercy to the nation of Israel must be taken seriously by the devout Bible student. Equally so, the exhortations of God with respect to His chastising of her!

With respect to the Land and people of Israel, and all the tribes of Arabia (promised through the seed of Ishmael in Genesis 17), God's character in being both a God of justice and a God of mercy, will prevail. The balance of these two divine attributes has somewhat baffled theologians for centuries. The great Jewish theologian, Saul of Tarsus, answered similar questions concerning God's election of Israel. His answer to many of them reiterated the words of the patriarch Moses, "I will have mercy on whom I will have mercy and I will have compassion on whom I will have compassion."

In other words a just God who is both one and at the same time a merciful God. This is the heart of the Gospel of Jesus Christ, the Jewish Messiah.

If you have become a 'new creature in Christ' (2 Corinthians 5:17), and have received the gift of His Holy Spirit into your life, then God has chosen you - chosen you in spite of you. Chosen you in spite of what you have negatively ever said, ever done, or ever thought - chosen you in spite of what, negatively, you ever will say, do, or think! It is called Amazing Grace.

In similar fashion God chose Israel - in spite of Israel - in spite of her past, her history, her transgressions, her lawlessness, her rebellions and her pride.

In Romans 11:29, the Bible says God's Call to Israel is 'irrevocable'. This means His words on the subject do not, and will not, change. In fact they will never change! They are both indelible and indestructible!

God will never revoke His unconditional promises to Israel.

Is it any wonder Paul, in writing, not to Jewish readers, but Gentiles (non-Jews), says in Romans 1:16, "I am not ashamed of the Gospel...it is the power of God unto salvation...First for the Jew, and (only) then to the Gentile."

In other words, the efficacy of Jesus' life and death upon the cross was primarily for the salvation of the Jewish people. He is their Messiah by promise. He is ours by grace. They are 'the vine', and we non-Jews, have been grafted into the vine as 'branches'.

When Jesus spoke to the woman at the well in John 4, He made a powerful, definitive statement, as He was often wont to do, "Salvation is of the Jews."

The woman was not Jewish, but a Samaritan. If you recall, the two peoples had no dealings with each other whatsoever. What was Jesus actually saying? That in order to receive salvation one had to become Jewish? Hardly. Such a possibility would bring into question the authenticity and veracity of the majority of Paul's writings. In short, most of the New Testament. Was He saying that in order to be saved, one had to keep the Jewish Law(s)?

Hardly.

If this were so, it makes a total mockery of the tremendous Pauline teaching given us in the New Testament concerning grace and the fact that 'by works of the law shall no man be made justified'-Romans.3:20

Jesus was surely declaring that salvation, or the means of, would emanate (come out of, or from) the Jewish race. Jesus of Nazareth declared Himself to be, "….the Way, the Truth, the Life. No man comes unto God the Father except by/ through Me." (John 14:6) Virtually the entirety of Matthew Chapter 1, gives us the human genealogy of Yeshua. His ancestral line was purely and exclusively Jewish.

Therefore we might ask, do these truths imply that the message of the Gospel (Good News) is therefore exclusively for Jewish people? Jesus Himself by His words and deeds proclaimed otherwise.

He was one day confronted by an emissary from a Roman military leader, and was informed the soldier's servant was sick. Without any anger, resentment, racism or bitterness toward Israel's enemy, Jesus healed the servant, and then made a major pronouncement, "I have never seen such great faith as this –**NOT even in Israel** "

He was speaking of a Gentile believer – a Roman centurion. Throughout His three years' earthly ministry we have recorded in the Gospels numerous cases of Jesus' ministry to Gentile people.

John summed up the earthly purpose of his beloved friend in the following words in John 3:16, "For God so loved the world, that He gave His only begotten Son, that whosoever believes in Him, will not perish, but have eternal life."

God's character is the basis of His salvation. It is also the reason for the Cross of Christ.

God cannot be God unless He is true and consistent with His character of justice. When God gave Moses the Ten Commandments (the Decalogue) He was not so dumb as to think that men could keep them! Possessed of a sinful nature since Adam and Eve's mess-up in the Garden of Eden, it was, and is, impossible for man to keep the law!

God Himself provided the Passover Lamb, to be the Atoning sacrifice for sin.

In Jesus' death, justice and mercy would meet. He was, and is, the Good News (the Gospel). He alone gives earthly and eternal hope to both Jew and Gentile alike.

Only a unique nature (the 'God-Man') could qualify in fulfilling Old Testament prophecy concerning the 'Suffering Servant'. (Isaiah 53) Only a divine/human being could qualify as the long-promised Messiah, and Saviour of the world.

Yeshua (Jesus) WAS that Person.

CHAPTER 6

AUTHORITY

—꩜—

The word Authority is a word rarely used in today's world. I trust the reader will not find me too belittling of the word in the following statement. Nowadays, when it is used in the west, more often than not it appears to be somewhat confined to defining and describing why society's teenagers rebel, and what types of authority they rebel against.

Webster's dictionary defines authority as, "The power or right to give commands, enforce obedience, take action or make final decisions; jurisdiction; the position of one having such power or influence resulting from knowledge or prestige."

In reality, adherence to authority is the essence of all successful relationships. The Biblical Christian acknowledges that God is the supreme Head of all righteous authority. Without digressing, I think we would all agree that compliance with, and obedience to, such authority is a Christian's responsibility only on the condition that such authority is righteous!

Rebellion against authority fuels unsuccessful relationships. To abuse righteous authority underlies the majority of personal, national and international relationships. The word and its meaning have been so misconstrued it has resulted in the breakdown of the moral and spiritual fabric of our western society, including the Church of Jesus Christ.

The current generation in the west raves incessantly about 'rights', be it the 'rights' of individuals, employees, students, ethnic groups, or nations. Believing himself to be a law unto himself, man tenaciously fights for his demands.

If there is a single hallmark which constitutes the moral degeneration in our day, surely it must be our 'self-centredness'. A modern belief that the world of today revolves around me, mine, myself and I! Very few any longer acknowledge the author John Donne's belief that – 'no man is an island'.

It is impossible, however, to discuss the issue of Authority without addressing the issue of Morality. To do so would, most assuredly, be an oxymoron of the worst kind.

Please believe this author when he declares his heartfelt wish to write more extensively on the subject. However, to do so would navigate you, the reader, away from assimilating the truths concerning Replacement Theology.

I only mention the subject of Authority with one purpose in mind, to enable the reader to grasp the backcloth in the scene of our western world at the beginning of the 21st century. A scene in which the genuine Christian is asked to raise the flag of conservative belief in the Bible, and to do so against the advocacy of Replacement Theology. The overwhelming outcome will inevitably witness a diminishing of anti-Semitism in our time, and in the time to come.

The demise and eventual collapse of communism in the former Soviet Union and eastern Europe, the weakening of national socialism in Germany; the destabilization of democracy in Britain and America, has created a political and moral vacuum which has, by and large, been replaced by secular humanism.

That, in itself, is one thing. Supplement this with the proliferation of fundamental Islam, and one can gain a general picture of the present day moral and spiritual demise of our western civilization.

The common thread running through secular humanism and fundamentalist Islam is the emphasis upon MAN himself. Make no mistake about it, the accelerating implementation of Islam's Sharia Law is NOT the requirement of 'Allah', but rather the requirement of a MAN – the prophet Mohammed.

The result is, the general philosophy of the western world is capsulated in a very popular song written by Paul Anka, "I'll do it my way." Made famous by the legendary Frank Sinatra, the song encapsulates the thinking of this age, and, arguably, every age before him.

The result is, man's general philosophy today is, 'leave me to my own devices' - undoubtedly a motivating force from this age for the song's lyrics. In essence, Isolationism rules. It is so entrenched in our North American society the average resident is oblivious of even knowing his neighbour's name only two doors away!

Resorting to traveling outside of the home for entertainment has waned. Who needs to go to town when we can have an entertainment center in our own living room? Why bother with the bar? If one can bring the drinks into one's home, it's less expensive, by far. I do not need to venture out in inclement weather. Lastly, at least, I will not be challenging the 'drinking/driving' laws! (admittedly one of the positives.)

William Golding's novel, Lord of the Flies, was not written as prophetic prose, but that is exactly what it has proved to be. Take away the Absolutes in Judaeo-Christian morality, and man will live by his own relative standards of morality. No wonder the late brilliant writer Francis Schaeffer prophesied a time coming at the turn of the 21st century, when we would, in the west, be living in a 'post-Christian society'.

The prevalent moral vacuum, and resultant rebellion against both divine and human authority over the affairs of men, has only served, in this day, to epitomize the Biblical account of the first man's rebellion against authority in the Garden of Eden.

Unlike previous centuries when men everywhere lived, worked, fought and died based upon their belief system, today's man proudly proclaims his existentialism (a philosophical movement which claims that individual human beings have full responsibility for creating the meanings of their own lives)[14].

It is a belief in the individual person as a free and responsible agent determining his or her own development through acts of the will. The definition sounds almost plausible and acceptable, were it not for its atheism. Surely we need men and women who believe in being free and responsible, exercising their wills for the benefit of society, and to the Glory of the God who created and redeemed them?

In the 6th century B.C. the Jewish prophet, Jeremiah, in Chapter 17, Verse 9, encapsulates almost all of the philosophers' teaching on the human heart, "The heart is deceitful above all things and beyond cure." In the Amplified Bible it is, "The heart is deceitful above all things, and it is exceedingly perverse and corrupt and severely, mortally, sick! Who can perceive, understand, be acquainted with his own heart and mind?"

If ever the world in this 21st century is witnessing a rampant rebellion against decent people and civilized democratic society, it is evident in the prolific rise of fundamentalist Islam.

---

[14] "existentialism." ..."It tends almost always to be atheistic. To be responsible for one's acts is one thing,but,in the absence of any god, it is also the source of their feelings of dread and anguish "......Oxford Dictionary....2nd Edition...1996.

Not that there is so much harm in its numerical growth alone, but rather in the demonic, inhuman outworking of what is blindly called 'the one true religion'. The pivotal tragedy, I believe, is not so much the result of people actually believing its doctrine, but rather that they do so under enforced and violent constraint. In fundamentalist Islam there is no place or tolerance for anyone using his (and emphatically not her) individual mind to think. A reality made worse, this writer believes, owing to the decline and, indeed, demise of Christianity.

The legacy of the 18th - 20th century Christian Revivals, have, at the beginning of this 21st century, left a spiritual vacuum in the west. The only remaining visible memorial lies in the buildings of churches and chapels. Today they are home to bingo games and Islamic activities! It may give you a barometer reading on where 'christian' Britain is really at today!

Christian evangelists are somewhat obscure in a western world besotted by materialism. Recruits for Christian ministry and international missionary work are in major decline. Ministry and missionary organizations are collapsing exponentially through lack of financial stability.

As for Judaism, it is tarnished with the same brush as Israel. When the media isolates and berates Israel, then what is said and felt about that country, applies inevitably to Judaism also. If it did not, then world-wide anti-Semitism which attacks and destroys Jewish synagogues, schools, cultural centres and cemeteries would be extremely rare.

When it comes to the question of the 'rights' of Israel as a God-covenanted land and people, we are faced, not so much with a crisis in the world regarding this nation but, more importantly, a crisis in the Church concerning Israel! The God-given 'rights' of the Chosen People (the People of the Book) have been challenged by the majority of Christendom for two millennia.

Never was this fact more espoused in our time than it was in a major British Christian magazine in 1991. The highly successful magazine was entitled Restoration, and in the summer of 1991 attributed an entire article to the subject of "The Truth About Israel."

What is understood theologically by Replacement Theology is best described by reproduction of statements from that particular article:

> The Israeli claim to Palestine as a Jewish state by divine right is incorrect! Their continued enforcement of this claim, by military oppression, is unjust....the progressive revelation of Scripture makes it clear that today, God has only one people, and it is "The Church." We must not apply Old Testament prophecies to the State of Israel when Jesus, Peter and Paul radically redirected our thinking concerning the Covenants of Promise. They are now given directly to the Church. It is a mistake for Christians to exalt Israelis to the position of being God's chosen people.

It is ironic that shortly following the article's publication, the Magazine ceased to exist! I wonder why?

CHAPTER 7

NATURAL AND SPIRITUAL RESTORATION

—⁊⁊⁊—

With respect to the literal nation of Israel, it is evident from numerous statements and prophecies in the Bible, there is a definite divine order God has established for dealing with His ancient people.

In applying the basic rules of hermeneutics and Biblical exegesis, it is obvious God declares He will firstly restore the Jewish people back to the God-given land called Israel. Secondly, He will restore the Jewish people to Himself. And only in that order.

The physical restoration to the Land precedes Israel's spiritual restoration as a nation. No other nation in Scripture is accorded a 'national salvation', save that of Israel only. The prophet Ezekiel, in Chapter 36 of his prophecy, spoke of God giving Israel, "a new heart and a new spirit."

This divine order of 'physical' preceding 'spiritual' is attested by the historical significance of two miracles in the 20th century. First, the miracle of the establishment of the modern state of Israel on May 14, 1948. The United Nations voted to give world Jewry a State and Homeland of its own, to be named - ISRAEL.

It was somewhat ironic that the motion to grant Israel Statehood was moved by the Russians, and passed with a majority of one!

David Ben-Gurion, as the new State's first Prime Minister, stood on the steps of Tel Aviv's Town Hall and declared the name of this 'new' country - Israel.

Second, the miracle of the re-unification of Israel's capital city, Jerusalem, in June 1967. It was the first time the Holy City was totally back in the hands of the Jewish people since its decimation by Titus, the Roman Emperor, in A.D. 70. David's city experienced many more destructive conquests in the ensuing centuries

Since 1948, and predominantly in the late 1980's and 1990's, floods of international Jews have been 'making aliyah' - returning to the land of Israel – the only true home-land for the Jewish people. Arguably, the only place in the world they will feel truly 'safe' and, contrary to the view of many, BE truly safe!

This fulfillment of Scripture in Isaiah 11:11-12 (referred to as 'the second great exodus'), is further proof that Israel's spiritual restoration is imminent.

Before the destruction of the temple in A.D. 70, the Jewish Rabbi, Saul of Tarsus, (later called Paul), wrote a letter to the church in Rome. In it, he declared the restoration to the Land and ensuing salvation of the people of Israel would be likened unto a "...resurrection from the dead." (Romans 11:15)

For the rest of us (Gentiles by birth and race), the news is equally exciting. These 'modern' events herald the imminent coming of the Messiah. The Psalmist wrote in Psalms 102:16, "For the Lord has built up Zion; He has appeared in His glory."

The prophet Zechariah says it will happen when the Jewish people are once again living in Jerusalem. "And I will pour out on the house of David and the inhabitants of

Jerusalem a spirit of grace and supplication. They will look on me, the one they have pierced, and they will mourn for him as one mourns for an only child, and grieve bitterly for him as one grieves for a first-born son." (Zechariah 12:10)

"The whole land, from Geba to Rimmon, south of Jerusalem, will become like the Arabah. But Jerusalem will be raised up and remain in its place, from the Benjamin Gate to the site of the First Gate, to the Corner Gate, and from the Tower of Hananel to the royal winepresses. It will be inhabited; never again will it be destroyed. Jerusalem will be secure." (Zechariah 14:10-11)

In conclusion, the implications of Replacement Theology taking a central place in the belief system of the Christian Church, affects history, past, present and future. The past we cannot change. By understanding the past, we can be educated anew in the present. My present understanding of these truths did not begin until I was 35 years of age. The Future? Thank God it is His problem. I do not say this lightly. Contrary to common belief, this is not a 'cop out'. However, I do believe I AM responsible to act according to the knowledge I have.

For some of you, this may be the very first teaching you have heard concerning the truth about Replacement Theology. The implication in believing and accepting Replacement Theology is truly frightening.

What if God were to be a God who changes His mind at will? **_Supposing_** He does this, revoking all His promises to Israel? **_Supposing_** all of these promises and prophecies were intended for the Christian Church instead? **_Supposing_** all of these words given to the nation of Israel have now, since the first coming of Jesus Christ, become redundant to the Jew, and, instead, are intended exclusively for the Christian believer to inherit?

If this were so, what ***assurance*** could we possibly have that God has not changed His mind about His promise to send the Messiah to earth for a second time?

God has given a multitude of promises in the Scriptures. One of these is the unequivocal assurance the coming Messiah will plant His feet upon the Mount of Olives in Jerusalem, Israel – there - and nowhere else! "On that day his feet will stand on the Mount of Olives, east of Jerusalem, and the Mount of Olives will be split in two from east to west, forming a great valley, with half of the mountain moving north and half moving south." (Zechariah 14:4)

In the light of this verse, it was no surprise to me to discover some years ago that Holiday Inns of America recruited architects to research the viability of erecting a hotel on the Mount of Olives, only to abandon the project in the light of discovering a geological fault running right through the middle of the mountain!

To take a text out of context and end up with a pretext is oscillating the basic rules of Biblical interpretation. In doing this, we then become adherents to situational ethics! That is, I make Scripture fit into whatever doctrine, circumstance or situation I want it to! Thereby, I can twist and turn God's teaching at will, find individual verses to support my own carnal beliefs, and, basically, make Scripture sub-servient to whatever context my own flesh demands!

This writer believes Replacement Theology is a deceptive tool, and has been for hundreds of years.

It is carnal and self-seeking in its appeal - many would define it as even 'racist'.

So many Christians, throughout the history of the Church, have become gullible. They somehow conclude that, to reject Replacement Theology and believe the Bible literally, would label them 'heretics'.

For example, they ask: "How can anyone (e.g. a Jew) receive salvation outside of the blood of Jesus Christ?";

"How can anyone enter heaven, ignoring or by-passing the cross?"

Paul makes it clear in Romans 2:29 that the answer to both questions is, they cannot. It is a mystery, a divine mystery.

We would do well to align ourselves with those called to be "Watchmen" as the Jewish prophet Isaiah exhorts in Chapter 62, "Take no rest for yourselves and give Him no rest until He establishes and makes Jerusalem a praise on the earth." But for the true believer in the Messiah (both Gentile and Jew), the 'divine mystery' regarding this miraculous spiritual salvation, has to be profoundly more intellectually intricate, than the 'mystery' of Israel's physical re-birth in the land God promised her.

As stated previously, every relationship the Creator has initiated with His creation, man, has been entered into on the basis of Covenant. A Biblical Covenant was always initiated by God, never by man.

Those who promulgate Replacement Theology either do not understand this consistent Biblical truth, or, deliberately choose to ignore it!

The Covenant, commonly referred to as 'the Abrahamic Covenant', is found in Genesis 12:1-4:

> Now the Lord said to Abram: "Get out of your country, From your family, And from your father's house, To a land that I will show you. I will make you a great nation; I will bless you, And make your name great; And you shall be a blessing. I will bless those who bless you, And I will curse him who curses you; And in you all the families of the earth shall be blessed." So Abram departed as the Lord had spoken to him, and Lot went with him. And Abram was seventy-five years old when he departed from Haran.

This Scripture affirms God's intention to bless the world with redemption, and to implement His eternally ordained plan through the exclusive medium of the nation of Israel.

As my dear friend Malcolm Hedding points out, 'The Abrahamic Covenant' is one covenant having three vital elements:

1. It declares a strategy – to reach the world through the nation of Israel.
2. It bequeaths a land – as an everlasting possession to Israel.
3. It gives a promise – to bless those who bless Israel, and to curse those who curse her.[15]

Malcolm uses the excellent 'visual aid' of a coin having three elements, a rim, a head side and a tail side. It remains one coin and it cannot be separated. It is impossible to deny, remove or ignore just one of the elements. The same must be applied to the Abrahamic Covenant. If God's promises to Israel have failed, then equally His promises to bless the world have also failed.

"On the same day the Lord made a covenant with Abram, saying: 'To your descendants I have given this land, from the river of Egypt to the great river, the River Euphrates – the Kenites, the Kenezzites, the Kadmonites, the Hittites, the Perizzites, the Rephaim, the Amorites, the Canaanites, the Girgashites, and the Jebusites.'" (Genesis 15:18-21)

God made a solemn promise of the Land of Canaan to Abraham. He affirmed this Divine Oath, "He remembers His covenant forever, the word which HE commanded, for a thousand generations, the covenant which He made with Abraham, and His oath to Isaac, and confirmed it to Jacob,

[15] Malcolm Hedding...."Christian Action for Israel"...4th Quarter... Newsletter...1999....Natal, South Africa.

for a statue, to Israel as an everlasting covenant." (Psalm 105:8-10)

It is hard (if not impossible!) to spiritually apply this passage to the Church! In Verse 8 the Bible says, "He remembers His covenant forever, the word He commanded for a thousand generations."

This can only speak of the perpetuity of God's promise. If one generation lasted only 40 years, it would make the territorial promise to Israel a 40,000-year lease! Words used in this passage (and others cited in this book), such as covenant, oath, decree, and everlasting covenant, if they have any meaning at all, must surely declare that God's will is for Israel to possess the Land of Canaan.

The prominent writer in the New Testament is a Jew by the name of Sha'ul (Saul), whose name was changed to Paul at the point of his becoming a follower of Jesus. Though Jewish he was also a Roman citizen and therefore God used him mightily in laying the foundation of His kingdom on earth.

It was Paul who wrote to Timothy and declared, "ALL Scripture is given by inspiration of God." (2 Timothy 3:16)

On this understanding, we find overwhelming Scriptural evidence for the place of Israel in the plan of God for the salvation of the human race.

Appreciating we live in a world today in which the visual appears to be of greater importance than the written word, I am prepared to concede that only the most diligent, disciplined and determined 'student' will take the time to open the Bible and check out the following references. It is not essential you do compare my notes with God's Word itself, but it will certainly benefit you if you do. For me, the writer, it is vital I defer and refer to an authority outside of myself. I choose that authority to be the Word of God – the Bible. To that end I have deliberately chosen not to write out the

Bible passages in full, but rather to encourage my reader to exercise those finger muscles!

A. God's Plan for Israel

God's purpose for Israel has always depended upon His initiative and election, and upon Israel's response as a righteous nation. (Deuteronomy 7) Israel is promised abundant blessing when living in a righteous relationship with God. (Leviticus 26:1-13 and Deuteronomy 28:1-14)

When the nation rebelled, it is important to know that God promised discipline, not rejection. (Leviticus 26:14-46 and Deuteronomy 26:15-68)

The dispersions of A.D. 70 and A.D. 135 led to 2000 years of exile. Scattering among the nations was the ultimate disciplinary measure with the promise of re-gathering to fulfill His purpose to the ultimate. (Deuteronomy 30)

HaShem (God) promised David a royal dynasty which, down the road, would reach eternal dimensions in the birth of Israel's Messiah. (2 Samuel 7:11-17 and 1 Chronicles 17:10-15)

The Gospel writer Matthew demonstrates that Jesus of Nazareth is the Messiah. (Matthew 1:1-16) It is revealed to the writer John that, after Jesus' death and resurrection, the Nazarene is still the Davidic King of the Jews. (Revelation 5:5 and 22:16)

When God promised the New Covenant to the Jewish people in Jeremiah 31:31, He not only described the nature of this Covenant, but also promised there would be a day when the Jewish people, "will all know me, from the least of them to the greatest," and, in this, they would be righteous:

But this is the covenant that I will make with the house of Israel after those days, says the Lord; I will put My law in their minds, and write it on their hearts;

and I will be their God, and they shall be My people. No more shall every man teach his neighbour, and every man his brother, saying, "Know the Lord," for they all shall know Me, from the least of them to the greatest of them, says the Lord. For I will forgive their iniquity, and their sin I will remember no more. (Jeremiah 31:33-34)

Such a Covenant like this, God had not previously initiated.He is here offering to His Chosen People an absolution which only GOD HIMSELF was qualified to effect. It was a Covenant securing for the believing Jew.....an intimate, personal, knowledge of Himself......a knowledge of His laws within their hearts....and an absolution of their past, present AND future sins for all eternity.

It was a Covenant God ALONE would make.........one He had already made in eternity....with His "only begotten Son, Yeshua(Jesus) ".........and now its benefits are being offered primarily to the Jewish people.

In my research into Jewish and Christian history over the last two millennia, I believe the Holy Spirit enabled me to perceive an interesting pattern throughout the 20th century. Important events in the physical history concerning Israel appeared to find a corollary in the spiritual history of the Christian Church.

Allow me to explain. The Azusa Street Revival was a Pentecostal series of meetings commencing on April 14, 1906 at the African Methodist Episcopal Church, Los Angeles, California. It was spearheaded by an African American preacher by name of William J. Seymour, and it lasted until 1915. Although heavily criticized at the time by secular media and certain theologians, it is considered by historians to be the primary catalyst behind the spread of Pentecostalism in the 20th century. The corollary of this is that, under the leadership of Theodor Herzl, a Hungarian Jew

(1860-1904), forces were working in Europe at the end of the 19th century to prepare the groundwork for the creation of a modern state called Israel. Britain, at that time holding the mandate to control Palestine, heard the cries of European Jewry, and in 1917 its Foreign Secretary, Lord Balfour, produced a report urging "...the creation of a national home-land for the Jewish people."[16]

A second significant act of God occurred midway through the 20th century. In the early 1950's, a South African preacher emerged, by name of David DuPlessis. Not only did he teach on the availability of the baptism and fullness of the Spirit for every seeking believer, but miracles were also performed through this man's ministry. Wherever DuPlessis preached, His ministry was accompanied by mighty outpourings of the Holy Spirit upon people. Multitudes thronged to hear him; multitudes were converted to Christ and healed. The corollary of this is the historical creation of the modern State of Israel in 1948. Many commentators, both then and since, would testify to this event also being considered 'miraculous'.

A further perceivable similarity would identify the amazing international outpouring of God's Spirit upon people of all Christian denominations in the 1960's. It became labelled as 'The Charismatic Movement' and swept through Christendom worldwide, seemingly with little respect for denominational labels or differences. As such, arguably, its most significant impact was that which took place within the Roman Catholic Church.

Regardless of outside opinions differing amongst Christians, it is an unequivocal fact that it paved the way for Catholics to be 'allowed', and encouraged, to read the Bible for themselves; something indisputably 'taboo' before. The corollary is that one of the greatest 'miracles' in history occurred in June 1967. For the first time in over 2,000 years,

---

16

a re-unified Jerusalem was back in the hands of its rightful 'leaseholder' - the Jewish people of Israel.

I share this as a confident subjective conviction (and therefore open to debate), but, admittedly, I am one of God's 'peculiar' people who believe the parallels between the Biblical 'Natural' and the Biblical 'Spiritual' are much closer than we sometimes dare to imagine. If not, I do not think our Creator/Redeemer would have designed a soul to enter into His prime creation, made that soul's shell from the dust of the earth, indwell that body/soul with His own spirit and call him 'Man'.

The Bible clearly declares the essence of God, "God is Spirit, and those who worship Him must worship Him in spirit and in truth." (John 4:24)

Speaking of 'the man of the earth' (Adam), and 'the second man from heaven' (Jesus), the Jewish writer Paul takes great pains in 1 Corinthians 15 to compare and contrast the 'natural' and the 'spiritual'. He does this, NOT with the objective to demonstrate their marked differences, but rather to declare their proximity to each other!

Such correlation between 'Natural' and 'Spiritual' is nowhere more poignantly observed than in the Book of the Old Testament prophet, often referred to as 'the Jewish prophet of the Spirit' - Ezekiel. It has been stated by the theologians that Chapter 37 is about 'the Spirit'. This observation, in, of all places, the Old Testament, pleases the Body of Christ, the Church, who believe the key theology of the Church is a theology of the Spirit. Other theologians, most notably Jewish ones, observe this Chapter to be about the nation of Israel, and this definitely pleases the Jew.

As a Gentile, I might surprise some of my readers with my own conviction when I apply the dictum by which I engage in hermeneutics (Remember? "A text without a context is a pretext"), and therefore I believe this passage of God's Word is primarily a prophecy concerning the land and people of

Israel! Remove the visors of 'spiritualization' and you will see in Scripture exactly why I believe this.

However, I want to express something exceedingly more important than whether this Chapter is about the Church, the Spirit, or Israel. Meditate on it carefully and prayerfully, and you will see it is a Chapter primarily about God Himself - what is near and dear to His heart. If ever a passage of Old Testament Scripture reveals the Trinitarian operation of the Godhead, it is Ezekiel 37. It begins with the Spirit (Ruach HaKodesh). It reveals the love of God (HaShem) for His covenant people – Israel. It closes with the coming of Jesus (Yeshua) for His own people - great David's Greater Son, the Messiah of Israel.

It was indeed the ancient prophet Ezekiel, through whom God revealed and confirmed His purpose with respect to Israel's future. Referring to Israel's restoration in Chapter 36 alone, God is described 14 times as the "Sovereign Lord," and it is He alone who declares 22 times, "I will do it."

The God of the nation of Israel, states what HE will do:

1. He will judge the nations for their treatment of Israel. (Ezekiel 36:3-7)
2. He will re-gather Israel to the land He promised... a land which will prosper and be rebuilt. A land in which His covenant-people will dwell in security. (Ezekiel 36:8-15)
3. He will judge Israel for "shedding blood" in the land, for preferring idols, and for "profaning God's name among the nations." (Ezekiel 36:16-21)
4. He will make Israel righteous for the sake of His holy name, NOT for Israel's sake. (Ezekiel 36:22)
5. As a result of Israel's righteousness, God will demonstrate to the nations that He is the Lord. (Ezekiel 36:23-28)

6. When all this has occurred, Israel will know rich spiritual and material blessing. (Ezekiel 36:29-38) A promise which the Apostle Paul succinctly describes as, "life from the dead." (Romans 11:15)

B. God Has no Plan to Replace Israel

Let us consider merely three of the 141 promises given us concerning Israel's return to the Land. I ask the proponents of Replacement Theology to consider just these alone and, in doing so, ask themselves the question, "How could these words possibly be transferred to the Christian Church?"

1. "Only if the heavens above can be measured, and the foundations of the earth below be searched out will I reject all the descendants of Israel for all they have done." (Jeremiah 31:37)
2. "I will surely gather them from the lands where I banish them...I will bring them back to this place... they will be my people and I will be their God. I will give them singleness of heart and action so that they will always fear me for their own good...I will make an everlasting covenant with them: I will never stop doing good to them, and I will inspire them to fear me, so that they will never turn away from me. I will assuredly plant them in their land with all my heart and soul." (Jeremiah 32:37-41)
3. "Have you noticed what these people are saying, 'The Lord has rejected the two kingdoms (i.e. Judah and Israel) he chose'? So they despise my people and no longer regard them as a nation. This is what the Lord says: 'If I have not established my covenant with day and night, and the fixed laws of heaven and earth, then I will reject the descendants of Jacob and David my servant, and will not choose one of his

sons to rule over the descendants of Abraham, Isaac and Jacob. For I will restore their fortunes and have compassion on them.'" (Jeremiah 33:24-26)

If words carry any meaning at all and Scripture is interpreted literally (i.e. when its context is literal), and NOT allegorical? If in our understanding of the Bible, one executes the centuries understanding of basic hermeneutics by comparing Scripture with Scripture? If God does not speak in indecipherable riddles? THEN these promises MUST guarantee a spiritual and territorial future for the Jews, and in no way make room for their replacement by any other people.

It was intended by the Author for even a child to understand it. As such, it deals a death blow to both factions represented in the Replacement Theology camp. Such a plain, simple, exegesis of the Bible is how God has designed His Word to be known, understood, broken, divided and used.

CHAPTER 8

REJECTION AND ACCEPTANCE

—〰—

"He was despised and rejected by men, a man of sorrows, and familiar with suffering." (Isaiah 53:3)

Having been a child of God since my conversion to Jesus Christ on May 13, 1960 I am sure the reader can appreciate, not how many messages I have preached, but how many more I have heard from the lips of others. I count it a privilege to have lived and sojourned in a number of countries, and an even greater blessing to have sat at the feet of some of the most anointed preachers of the last century.

Out of the treasury of those messages I heard, there is one that stands out more memorable than all the others. Being no different from any other mortal human being, I experienced 'wounds and bondages' from childhood and adolescence. I well recall the sermon God used most poignantly in ministering to the deepest of my emotional pain, the pain of rejection!

It was delivered on Sunday, the 25th September at a seminar of the 1983 Feast of Tabernacles (Sukkot). This annual event in David's Holy City of Jerusalem is annually convened by the International Christian Embassy . The modern celebration of this ancient Jewish Feast has, since 1980, witnessed an escalation in attendance, from 500 to over 7,000 Bible-believing Christians gathered from over 80 nations coming up to Jerusalem to worship. It ranks as the largest 'tour' group annually to visit Israel - a notable fact considering the uncertain times for this fledgling nation.

The speaker that Sunday was the internationally renowned Derek Prince (now deceased). Kenyan born, British educated, and a resident of both Israel and the United States. As Derek preached, my eyes became watery, the mist became gentle tears and before long, the tears had metastasized into relentless sobs. My being a 36-year-old adult male was irrelevant. The Holy Spirit (Ruach HaKodesh in Hebrew) was, through this message, performing surgery deep within my heart, soul and emotional being.

I recall only two things Derek Prince said that day.

First, was his reading of the well-known passage in Isaiah 53, the classic prophetic description of the Suffering Servant of God, given us by the Jewish prophet 800 years before Jesus' birth.

Second, Derek declared a statistic taken, not only from his own lifelong ministry, but also from the research work of a vast multitude of preachers, therapists and psychologists. It was this - as high as 75% - 80% of all peoples suffer in one form or another from the malady of REJECTION. Personally speaking, I would put this figure much higher!

One year to the month before hearing this message in Jerusalem, I experienced the life-changing encounter with the living God in Galilee (referred to earlier in this book). It was then, you may recall, God gave me, for the first time, a consciousness of just how deeply this spiritual and emotional sickness of rejection was controlling my life as an adult.

Yet, at one and the same time my 'suffering' was as God told me that night, "a necessary pre-requisite for the work to which I am calling you." The Lord plainly told me that, without it (rejection) it would be impossible for me to identify with Israel and the Jewish people. Even then, such identification would be miniscule in comparison to the rejection experienced by them.

It was my initial desire to label this Chapter "David and Bathsheba." It appeared inconsistent with the main theme of the book, yet, I was convinced the Lord was revealing to me some profound truths to share with the Body of Christ. In my spirit, I knew He was revealing HIS lessons for the learning from this legendary Israeli king's indiscreet love affair. Lessons for us, His children, which shed much light upon God's present and future relationship with His ancient chosen people.

Yet again, God was asking one of His servants (on this occasion, me!) to do something seemingly incomprehensible and write about David's paramount sinfulness as the subject of this book's final Chapter!

You may well ask, what does **the story of David and Bathsheba possibly have to do with Replacement Theology?** Writing this Chapter on "David and Bathsheba" was to me....somewhat akin to Noah building a boat in the desert, Abraham killing his divinely-promised heir, or Elijah pouring water on a fire before lighting it!

Every one of them an oxymoron!

Each of the above cited Biblical colossus were spiritual giants,...at least, that is what my Sunday School teacher taught me 55 years ago!

Oxymoron or not, in the end it did not matter. I changed the title to 'Rejection and Acceptance' ! Yet it is the understanding and discernment of Scripture which is given, not only for our learning, but, above all, for our edification.

I love the Biblical account of the life of David – arguably Israel's greatest king. It took me half a lifetime to unlearn what I had learnt from those unwitting Sunday School teachers half a century back. I discovered these Biblical 'giants' to be tainted and polluted by the ravages of sin and the mortality of the human condition...... none more so than King David himself.

My intelligence and, highly arguable, genius (!!) has attempted a multitude of ways to comprehend the relationship between Israel's king, and Israel's God. It is called 'trying to comprehend a problem in the natural'.

But the Christian is called to 'discern in the area of the spiritual and super-natural'!

"How is it possible," I asked, "for God to define this shepherd boy as, uniquely, 'a man after God's own heart?'"

"Absurd!" we scream; "Impossible," "unjust," "unfair," we cry out. How could a holy, righteous and morally pure God accept a king like this?

Here is David – the deceiver, the adulterer, the murderer........ greed and envy gripping his flesh as he yields to the tempter's fiery darts. In one short evening of passion, Israel's king loses his self-respect.

He lights the torch of his own self-destruction and the consequences ensued:.... the death of his son, the decimation of his household, the onslaught of murder and intrigue in his family. For 'when a man plays - he pays!'

Yes, THIS IS 'a man after God's own heart'.

In 24 years of being a 'lover of Zion' (often referred to as 'Christian Zionist'), and loyal friend to Israel, Bible student, pastor and teacher, I had never grasped the power of some words of God, until I came to prepare this particular Chapter you are now reading.

In 2 Samuel 12:10, the prophet Nathan gives David his king, God's response to the monarch's sin with Bathsheba: "Now, therefore the sword will NEVER depart from your house...." How human and understandable it would be for David to turn against God in anger and contempt. Let's face it, he was the King of Israel.

How many of God's people become angry against Him when their lives or the lives of their loved ones are damaged and destroyed by the ravages of cancer, heart attack, disease, deprivation and death?

I am writing this Chapter on the back of receiving news that the 27-year-old son of a friend has just become a quadriplegic after a diving accident. Only two days after hearing this, my son told me of a young Christian couple in his church losing their 2-year-old daughter to a choking accident. How would you and I fare spiritually and emotionally, if told that our yet unborn son or daughter would die at birth?

And what was mortal David's response to all this? The twentieth Verse of this Chapter reveals to us exactly why God called David 'a man after My own heart'. The Bible said, 'he went into the house of the Lord and WORSHIPPED.'

This IS a man of God indeed.

So, you have every justification to ask, "What does the story of David's public humiliation possibly have to do with the subject of Replacement Theology?"

I offer it for the reader's thinking to emphasize three essential truths, NOT about man but, far more importantly, about the nature and character of God Himself.

First, IF, in order to be a recipient of God's blessings (nationally or individually) man must be obedient to a law or laws, no human being in the entire history of the planet could be blessed! If the Gospel does not teach unconditional grace, it teaches nothing.

Second, IF God could severely reprimand and discipline 'the man after His own Heart', YET, be true and faithful to His ancient covenant with David's forefather, Abraham, why would He be suddenly rebellious against His own nature in these last momentous days? Apart from numerous Scriptures predicting the return of Israel to her God-given land, three entire Chapters (9, 10 and 11) of Paul's letter to the Romans are occupied with the Apostle's teaching on both the physical and spiritual resurrection of the Jewish nation.

God HAD to be true to His own moral nature and, therefore, discipline David for his sin. BUT, He NEVER revoked His unconditional promise to David's ancestor, Abraham.

"ALL the land that you see I will give to you and your offspring forever. I will make your offspring like the dust of the earth, so that if anyone could count the dust, then your offspring could be counted." (Genesis 13:14-16)

It is not based upon anything else except His covenant love. God gave it, and only God can take it away.

As Malcolm Hedding states, "the deceptive half truth teaching of Replacement Theology makes a mockery of God's character for it rests upon the premise that IF you fail God in any way, He will discard you."[17] If this statement IS true of the character of Israel's God, then David was toast!

SO ARE YOU, AND SO AM I!

Far more importantly, IF God was finished with David, inevitably ALL that He planned for, in and through 'great David's greater Son (Jesus)' would also be finished! There would have been NO Messiah, NO Son of God, NO redemption, NO salvation.

We would be left only with a Jewish annual Day of Atonement (Yom Kippur), the need of which would not only be annual, but daily. A need to present 'offerings or sacrifices' to God, a constraint to perform 'good works', say enough prayers, log enough synagogue or church attendances. ALL performed in an attempt to BUY salvation - the tragedy of most sects and cults. Dare I set myself up for the inevitable 'readers theological firing-squad', and say, it is the tragedy also of many who profess to be 'Christian'!

This is why Jesus detested religion!

---

[17] Malcolm Hedding..."Christian Action for Israel"...4th Quarter Newsletter...1999.

Religion comes from the Latin word 'religare'; basically it means 'rules and regulations'.

Is it any wonder our Jewish friends have difficulty coming to simple faith in their Jewish Messiah, Yeshua? They have 614 rules and laws they believe they need to obey in order to receive salvation!

Their belief in the imperativeness of obeying them is ONLY because Judaism is entrapped by its own insistence to have its people live under the Mosaic covenant instead of the NEW COVENANT !

Religion is MAN trying to reach up to God. Christianity is GOD reaching down to man.

In a world in which our television newscaster says, "Good evening," and then proceeds to give us ten reasons why it is **not**, the Christian and Messianic believer is the only messenger of 'Good News' (Gospel) to our world.

The 'Good News' is quite simply..... a sovereign, righteous, holy, perfect God was not, and is not, taken by surprise at the sins of men and women. He tells us, "He chose us in Jesus before the creation of the world." (Ephesians 1:4)

That is, before the world was framed, before the first man was on the planet, before you and I were born.... BEFORE you and I consciously and wilfully lived out our human nature in thoughts, words and actions contrary to the character of God (called SIN, before modern man opted to discard it from usage in our time). Such is infinite knowledge and love.

Is it any wonder one of Jesus' followers, the doubting, questioning Jew named Thomas, uttered a cry no Orthodox Jew would ever utter of a mere man: "My Lord and My God." (John 20:28)

He was saying in Hebrew "Baruch HaShem Adonai"... you Yeshua (Jesus), you are both God and Lord.

Even sceptical, quizzical, disbelieving, Thomas, has, by grace alone, become like David, 'a man after God's own heart'.

The One who said, "I tell you the truth, until heaven and earth disappear, not the smallest letter, not the least stroke of a pen, will by any means disappear from the law (Torah) until everything is accomplished." (Matthew 5:18)

This is HIS truth.

It is this truth I declare fearlessly and aloud to the adherents and proponents of Replacement Theology.

My message is a message which declares, "Everything must be accomplished," which God spoke to the world through the prophets concerning Israel.

My heart cry to the Church is simply this: HEAR, and in this time, UNDERSTAND, what Paul the Jewish disciple of Jesus wrote to the Church in Rome: "I am not ashamed of the Gospel, because it is the power of God for the salvation of everyone who believes; FIRST, FOR THE JEW; then for the Gentile." (Romans 1:16)

God has never rescinded this exhortation! It is a commission to the Church which has never been revoked by God, ONLY by the majority of the Church.

We have, generally speaking, found the Jew somewhat stubborn and hard of heart when it comes to matters of the Gospel. Is it really any wonder to us believers this is so? Christianity has blamed their race for the death of Jesus, and, because of that belief, spent 2,000 years actively engaged in retribution toward Jesus' descendents after the flesh!

We are also without excuse when we declare ourselves 'Bible-believing' Christians, thus hinting we are not responsible for any failure in Jewish evangelism!

In Acts 10, we find this scenario in reverse.

We previously mentioned the Apostolic Church of the first century comprised mostly of Jewish believers in the Jewish Messiah, Yeshua, whom Gentiles call Jesus.

When Peter saw his vision in Joppa, of God descending from heaven in a blanket filled with animals, it was more than Peter could bear. Whether it included pigs or not (and possibly it did), this was certainly no flying, kosher, deli ! Peter was appalled!

Then he utters an oxymoron of the worst kind, worse than 'military intelligence', worse than 'an honest politician'. Peter yells at God ,

"NO, LORD." (Acts 10:14)

I find this to be very encouraging for me in my personal journey of faith !

Oh, how we Christians find it so easy to succumb to our lower nature, saying 'Yes' and 'No' to the Lord at whim, when His directives simply do not dovetail with our flesh!

TODAY, God is fulfilling his Word to every last jot and title, and He will do it regardless of how loud we rant and rave and say, "Yes" when we should say, "No" and "No" when we should say "Yes."

May God give us the wisdom and discernment to comprehend the truth about Replacement Theology, and, in humble penitence, ask God to give us HIS LOVE for HIS TRUTH, and consequentially, HIS LOVE for the Jewish people – "the apple of His eye" ..Zechariah 2:8 . This means that to God......His love for Israel is THE most sensitive part of His heart.

THIS IS HOW IMPORTANT ISRAEL IS TO YAHWEH,......

THE GOD OF ABRAHAM, ISAAC AND JACOB.

Rick Joyner, in his book HARVEST* summed up God's Truth powerfully, succinctly and beautifully,

"It is the consummation of the age when spiritual Israel and natural Israel become ONE NEW MAN in CHRIST."[18]

---

[18] Joyner, Rick...'Harvest'..Published by Whitaker House...1997New Kensington, PA.

The Greek word for 'Christ' is 'Christos'. It means 'Messiah or Anointed One'. If this is what the word 'Christ' means, what do you think the true meaning of the word 'Christ-ian' is?

It means, 'Anointed ones'!

David knew God in such intimate relationship, he was 'God's Anointed' for Israel at that time. Even after Nathan's stunning rebuke to him for his adultery he wrote a Psalm (51): "Surely I have been a sinner from birth, sinful from the time my mother conceived me" (verse 5). He follows up his declaration of this truth with a repeat of the word 'surely'; "Surely you desire truth in the inward part of me." (verse 6)

The truth about God's love for His chosen people is the truth that man is accepted, loved and forgiven (GRACE). The truth about GRACE is that we are given what we do **NOT deserve..** The truth about MERCY is,…. we are **NOT** given what we **DO** deserve!.....i.e.His judgment .

Jesus said, "You shall know the truth, and the truth will set you free." (John 8:32)

The truth about TRUTH is that man is able to contribute only one thing toward his salvation – the sin from which He is redeemed! The truth about SIN is, it blinds us to the TRUTH about God.

The truth about God is, God is LOVE. He loves 'the one new man.' (Ephesians 2:14) Jesus has made the two into ONE, and "…destroyed the barrier, the dividing wall of hostility" between Jew and Gentile.

He made peace through the cross, and reconciled them both to God. (Ephesians 2:15-16).

It (salvation/reconciliation/forgiveness) is FINISHED. The Messiah has come! HE IS my Yom Kippur.

When the citizens of Jerusalem traded the Jewish Messiah for a two-bit murderer and criminal 2000 years ago, they uttered an oath before Pontius Pilate- "his blood be upon our hands".

Their God heard and answered that cry.......and for 2000 years there has been **NO** Israel.

BUT GOD.....................was hearing and answering another prayer....offered by a Jewish Galilean as He breathed His last upon a blood-spattered Roman gibbet:-

"Father, FORGIVE THEM....for they know not what they do"

Today........there **IS AN ISRAEL.......and it is nothing short of a miracle.**

The "veil is lifting" from the Jewish eyes........it now needs to lift from the eyes of the Church. It is this author's prayer that this simple book might contribute toward that end.

Elohim, the God of the Bible, is **FAR** from being finished with Israel.............for she truly is .."**the apple of His eye".**

"Pray for the peace of Jerusalem"- Psalm 122v.6.

JERUSALEM

—∽∿—

Jerusalem, Jerusalem, All roads lead to you,
Jerusalem, Jerusalem, Your light is shining through.
You will show, show the way,
To all who see it shine,
So we can live in peace in Jerusalem this time.

The walls will keep you in,
The walls will keep you out
Its gates are tall and lone,
And know what it's about.

Jerusalem is old,
Jerusalem is new
Jerusalem can hold,

Moslem, Christian , Jew

The markets and the alleys,
The temples and the tombs
A place for all believers,
It has so many rooms.

Jerusalem, Jerusalem, All roads lead to you.
Jerusalem, Jerusalem, your light is shining through.
You will show, show the way
To all who see it shine,
So we can live in peace in Jerusalem, This time.

Song by Don McLean

Printed in the United States
129107LV00002B/28/P